M000298429

SATER DESIGN

SATER DESIGN

A

PORTFOLIO OF

30

LUXURY ESTATES

FROM ACCLAIMED DESIGNER

DAN F. SATER II, AIBD

The Sater Group, Inc.
The Center at the Springs
25241 Elementary Way, Suite 200
Bonita Springs, FL 34135

Dan F. Sater, II — *CEO and Author*

Rickard Bailey — *Editor-in-Chief*

Jennifer Emmons — *Editor*

Laura Hurst Brown, Words Et Cetera™ — *Writer*

Dave Jenkins — *Illustrator*

Diane J. Zwack — *Creative Director / Art Director*

CONTRIBUTING EDITORS

Laura Hurst Brown, Amy Fullwiler, Clare Ulik

GRAPHIC ARTISTS

Kim Campeau, Wayne Chambers, Emily Sessa

PLAN PRODUCTION

Darren Sumner — *Plan Production Coordinator*

Erin Bir, Nathan Fiegland, Ramiro Perez, Tom Starnes

CONTRIBUTING PHOTOGRAPHERS

Everett & Soulé, Dan Forer, Tom Harper, Joseph Lapeyra,

Kim Sargent, Laurence Taylor,

Doug Thompson, Oscar Thompson, CJ Walker

Cover Photography: CJ Walker

A DESIGNS DIRECT PUBLISHING BOOK

Printed by: Toppan Printing Co., Hong Kong
First Printing: February 2006
10 9 8 7 6 5 4 3 2

All floor plans, renderings, text designs and illustrative material
copyright © The Sater Group, Inc.
Entire publication copyright © 2006 Verandah Publishing, Inc. and may not
be reproduced by any means without permission.
No part of this publication may be reproduced in any form or
by any means — electronic, mechanical, photomechanical, recorded or
otherwise — without the prior written permission of the publisher.
ISBN hardcover: 1-932553-13-4

DEDICATION

I would like to

dedicate this collection

to my wife of twenty-two years, Debbie,

for her tireless behind-the-scenes

support and encouragement. Without her,

none of this would have been possible.

Dan F. Sater, II

Contents

Acknowledgements

This book has been a lifelong dream of mine: creating a portfolio to showcase a sampling of the thousands of custom homes created by The Sater Group in our twenty-year history. The firm's accomplishments would not have been possible without the efforts of our incredible team members, past and present. I would personally like to acknowledge Dave Jenkins and Diane Zwack, whose creative genius have made my homes look especially good. Additionally, I wish to thank Laura Hurst Brown — her writing skills and understanding of my design ideas have brought to word my thoughts previously unwritten.

I also would like to thank my client builders—whose foresight and courage allowed many of our concepts to become reality—as well as the interior designers, lighting professionals, landscape architects and others that make it all come together. I would especially like to thank Scott Windham, ASLA, my cohort and friend, whose creativity has played a crucial part in the success of my designs.

This book would not be possible without the tireless efforts of Rickard Bailey, my trusted publisher, consultant, advisor and friend. Thanks for your many years of advice, wisdom, encouragement and friendship.

Most importantly of all, I wish to thank my Lord and Savior, Jesus Christ. He has been my biggest source of inspiration as He truly is the greatest Designer ever.
Hebrews 3:4

Foreword
by William C. Steere, Jr.

Whatever else we wish them to be, our houses are principally places to live. Ten years ago, my wife Lynda and I discovered a narrow patch of ground on a tip of land jutting into a bend of the Imperial River, near Estero Bay. We set our minds on a scenario that would satisfy our need to retreat from the clamor of round-the-clock schedules yet facilitate our desire to entertain family and friends. We pictured wide interior spaces unencumbered by superfluous décor—every detail a partner of function, with few walls and easy transitions to the outdoors. Traveling abroad for many years had influenced our architectural tastes, and we had in mind an exterior style that would reflect our recollections of places far away.

Lynda and Bill Steere

Houses that take advantage of their settings are rare places today. We found intense peace in the fluid, inside-outside spaces of ageless homes hugging the coastal areas across the globe, and wanted to recreate that sense of serenity here—not with an archetype but with an evocative house that works with our everyday lives.

To build this home, we reasoned, would require an extraordinary mind, an experienced planner who would also understand the pure spirit and utter complexity of an essential retreat set in the 21st Century. Having already dismissed two other home designers, who claimed the lot was too small for the square footage we were looking for, we were fortunate to find Dan F. Sater II, who was undaunted by the lot's shape and size. He proceeded to draw up plans and orchestrate the building project from the ground up. True to the Sater design strategy, the house belongs to its site and functions flawlessly for our never-formal style. Every wall of the waterside perimeter opens to the outdoors, and the angled center of the home takes in views of the inlet and bay—just as we requested.

A place of one's own requires the right mix of contrast and balance, nature and civility, repose and diversity to suit the individual character of the owner. Dan Sater is the one who always gets it right.

William C. Steere, Jr., is Chairman of the Board Emeritus of Pfizer Inc., and Chairman of the Pfizer Foundation. Listed by **Forbes** *as one of America's Most Powerful People, Mr. Steere is Vice Chairman of the Board of the New York Botanical Garden, where, together with his wife Lynda, he created the Steere Discovery Center, a teaching facility for children.*
The William and Lynda Steere residence appears on pages 60-69.

Redefining "home"

Working for nearly thirty years in a rapidly growing area of Southwest Florida, Dan F. Sater II, AIBD, has redefined the way people live at home. Recognizing that we spend more time in our homes than we do in any other single place, Dan creates functional environments designed for everyday life: places to spend time with our families, relax, and entertain guests—shaping the very epicenter of our lives.

With today's diverse lifestyles, shouldn't home provide much more than just shelter? Why create spaces that simply impress, rooms that are inefficient or houses that are uninspiring and dull? In our fluid and fast-paced world, people must adapt to changing needs and make their home work for them in a wide variety of ways and settings. As envisioned by Dan, the new home certainly can impress, but more importantly it can soothe, give security, delight and even inspire its owners.

For over two decades, the challenge of redefining "home" has been the passion of The Sater Group and its partners: builders, landscape architects, interior designers and lighting professionals—all of whom share Dan's vision. Perhaps most important are the clients who put their trust in this team to create truly unique homes, the best of which are presented within these pages. These clients have come to understand, as have Dan and his team, that a home is much more than four walls, and have had the foresight, wherewithal and adventurous spirit to commit to making it happen.

The true art of luxury is the ability to weave together the client's vision and a blend of styles that maintain harmony with the site—the palette on which Dan creates a masterwork. Like that of an accomplished artist, Dan's passion resonates throughout his designs, reflecting in each home thoughtful details and dynamic features, like carefully placed strokes on a canvas.

In perfecting his techniques, Dan developed an organic style keyed to the site that breaks down the barriers between indoor and outdoor spaces. Evidence of this blurring of the lines between house and nature is found in Dan's signature disappearing-corner glass walls—an invention that has been widely recognized and imitated.

Dan's ability to bring together modern design with classical detailing is apparent in this portfolio of well-crafted homes. His diverse revival strategies grant his homes a unique character and persona—with derivative treatments that evoke centuries-old themes without replicating the original works. To some, this may seem an irreverent treatment of the past and our heritage, yet the process achieves inventive designs that nourish time-honored traditions while embracing contemporary floor plans and amenities that satisfy the owner's desires.

Like all true art, especially works that redefine a medium, Dan's designs invite lively discussion. Many love the homes and a few resist accepting some new turn in the vernacular and culture, but all are moved in some way. And that is what art does: offers the momentum of newly created works to broaden the common perspective—without obstructing the vision or impeding the view. And the view from and within these homes is truly phenomenal.

EARLY YEARS

BREAKING GROUND

Promising beginnings

The first years for The Sater Group were ones of self-discovery. Starting out as a drafting firm doing modifications for production builders, the Sater enterprise began to thrive as Dan started to express and develop his design concepts. He was most inspired by the works of architects such as Frank Lloyd Wright, Henry Hobson Richardson and Frank Furness, whose works were a reflection of their own unique architectural style and language. These pioneers understood and used accepted traditional design standards, but rather than being confined by them, they manipulated these same standards as necessary to accomplish their goals.

Many early Sater clients came from the northern states—to create a seasonal home and escape the harsh winters there. Dan responded to their appreciation for the local Gulf Coast climate by designing houses that not only captured but also embraced the beautiful tropical Florida environment—using open, flowing spaces in organic arrangements that connected easily with the outdoors. This strategy created flexible rooms that did not just overlook views but were immersed by them with scenery pouring in from every angle. A key idea in mastering this concept was the use of cornerless sliding-glass doors, which permit rooms to expand on two sides into wraparound verandas, multiplying the sense of space. More importantly, the rooms feel like outdoor cabanas, intimately in sync with nature.

Another challenge to design was the lifestyle of the clients. Unlike homes for growing and just-beginning families, these plans were drawn largely for empty-nester couples who entertained frequent visits by grown family members—with families of their own—and close friends. In such homes, privacy is an essential element, while intimacy and places to gather are vital components, and a sense of wide-open space is important for casual entertaining.

Responding to the diverse needs of couples in transition was a welcome challenge. Dan's explorations led to new designs that possessed unique character, with the clustering of interior spaces and immediate access to outdoor environments. Even better, Dan's designs offered the capacity for reinvention to suit the lifestyles of owners drawn to the ageless ebb of Florida's coastal regions.

Waterford

© THE SATER GROUP, INC.

Artistic spirit enlivens contemporary forms.

dan's notes | *This unique design focuses on the interplay of indoor and outdoor spaces, balancing contemporary elements—sweeping and concentric lines—with an organic aesthetic sense. Designed for a couple who likes to entertain, the home offers many great places for people to gather in small, conversational groups. Even the grand, open spaces feel intimate and inviting, and many rooms lead outside. For me, the dining room is the focal point of the house: set in a suspended canopy over a glass bay surrounded by a koi pond—a buffered space cantilevered over a meditative water garden. Here, the environment is spectacular yet still airy and quiet.*

Drawn as a conceptual plan that was later built, this contemporary Mediterranean-style home manifests a wealth of cutting-edge components merged with an inviting sense of intimacy. Designed for entertaining, the formal heart of the home draws the eye toward spectacular rear views. Just off the foyer, a winding staircase links to an upper-level guest suite and deck, while a side gallery leads to a dramatic dining room carved into a mitered-glass bay. The varied shapes of the plan meander over the landscape, creating marvelous encounters with scenery and light. A sun deck overlooks the fairway, pool and spa.

LOCATION:
BONITA SPRINGS, FLORIDA

BUILDER: LIFESTYLE CONCEPTS

LANDSCAPE ARCHITECT:
SMALLWOOD DESIGN GROUP

INTERIOR DESIGN:
RICHARD GEARY INTERIORS

PHOTOGRAPHY BY:
OSCAR THOMPSON

dining room | The bold curvature of the mitered-glass panels surrounding the formal dining room extends the spatial boundaries of the home and brings in a sense of the outdoors. A series of transoms patterned with grillwork defines the outer limits of the space, and heralds the transition between indoor and outdoor elements of the home. Open to scenes of the motorcourt, the room also permits glimpses of a koi pond, which wraps the front of the home with a lush perimeter.

dining room twilight | In harmony with its site, the glass turret harboring the dining room juts over the koi pond, hovering serenely above the water and embracing the beauty of the outdoors. A model of organic architecture and an engineering masterpiece, with its seemingly unsupported circular canopy roof, the space functions as a temple of natural light. The room and its setting are interwoven, with the interior space reflecting the variations of light and scenery, even at dusk.

family room | Contemporary lines frame sweeping views of the pool, veranda and fairway in the leisure room, which opens through retreating glass doors to outdoor seating and an alfresco kitchen. Cypress planks line a cove-vaulted ceiling, which increases the dimensions of the interior space. A corner fireplace features a sleek granite surround, and an ebonized media center features a glass panel that, when opened, conceals the lighted display cabinet.

rear view | The strong interplay of angles and lines creates a showcase of organic composition at the rear perimeter. Curved forms shape the pool environment, reflecting light from many sides of the interior. Contemporary quoined columns support a covered veranda with a soaring ceiling—an architectural enhancement created by concealing the support beams within the sundeck floor—permitting an open, unimpeded flow to the outdoor living area. Intricate grillwork lines the deck overlooking the pool and rear property. Glass walls in the leisure room retreat to link the indoor and outdoor sitting spaces, while floor-to-ceiling windows bring in views.

Waterford | SATER EARLY YEARS

site plan | Organic elements define the archetypal design, structured with clean lines and a contemporary approach that prevails throughout the home. At the core of the plan, the grand foyer and formal living space overlap in an open arrangement that brings in spectacular vistas and increases circulation at the hub. A side gallery forms an axial relationship to the public realm toward the fairway and creates a dramatic procession through the home. The owners' retreat features a garden bath with views of the koi pond through a curved wall of glass. Separate guest suites offer luxe privacy.

rear view | The sculpted edges of the spa, wader and pool create a free-flowing pattern of concentric lines.

site plan legend

1 COVERED ENTRY
2 GRAND FOYER
3 LIVING ROOM
4 STUDY
5 DINING ROOM
6 MASTER BATH
7 MASTER SUITE
8 HER WARDROBE
9 HIS WARDROBE
10 WET BAR
11 POWDER BATH
12 BREAKFAST NOOK
13 PANTRY
14 KITCHEN
15 LEISURE ROOM
16 GUEST SUITE #1
17 GUEST BATH #1
18 LOFT
19 POOL BATH
20 OUTDOOR KITCHEN
21 COVERED VERANDA
22 POOL
23 SPA
24 DECK
25 UTILITY ROOM
26 GUEST BEDROOM #2
27 GUEST BATH #2
28 FOUNTAIN
29 STUDIO/GUEST
30 STUDIO/GUEST BATH
31 KOI POND
32 2-CAR GARAGE
33 MOTOR COURT

1ST FLOOR

© The Sater Group, Inc.

© The Sater Group, Inc.

Open to Below

2ND FLOOR

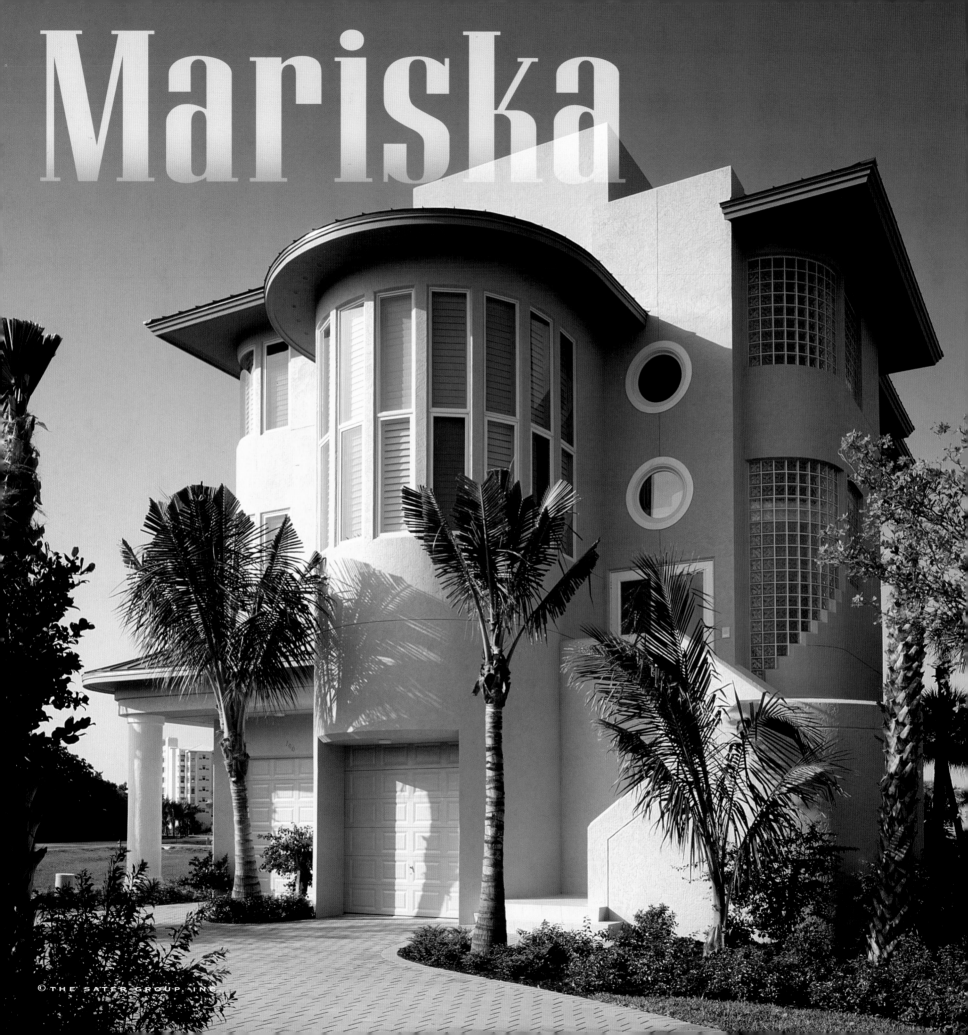

Mariska

© THE SATER GROUP, INC.

Dramatic seafront manor takes on a mid-century Art Moderne theme.

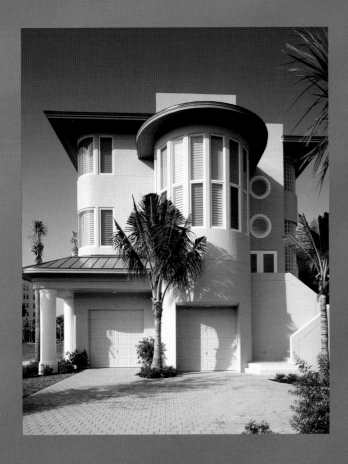

dan's notes | *Various modern stylists inspired the theme of this home, primarily the works of Le Corbusier, who connected the use of expressive sculptural forms with the function of houses. The plan extends toward the Gulf and employs curved walls of glass and retreating doors to bring in views. The elevation was raised extensively to accommodate the narrow lot and conform to seaside regulations, which increased the vertical scale of the home. To overcome this, I added curvilinear elements to the perimeter—a wide deck, winding stairwell and a loggia—to subdue the massing and increase the texture of the streetscape.*

Curved masonry walls and a teal standing-seam roof interpret mid-century modern architecture with an individual look that takes in the cool, contemporary informality of the beach locale. The more minimalist sensibility of the interior establishes the serene tone required of a getaway, with large-scale spaces that are both carefully defined and gracious. Clean lines and panels of glass contribute to the sculptural quality of the home, enhancing the unrestrained nature of the plan and framing powerful views of the Gulf of Mexico. Bridges and catwalks link private retreats and vaulted spaces that reach into the upper level and curved windows fill the rooms with natural light. Oriented to the rear of the home, the living room, breakfast nook, dining room and kitchen enjoy views that extend to the horizon.

LOCATION: NAPLES, FLORIDA

BUILDER: LONDON BAY HOMES

LANDSCAPE ARCHITECT:
SMALLWOOD DESIGN GROUP,
SCOTT WINDHAM, ASLA

INTERIOR DESIGN:
JAN WALLACE, ROBB & STUCKY

PHOTOGRAPHY BY:
OSCAR THOMPSON

25

dining room | Located at the center of the plan, the formal dining room connects the foyer, hall and primary living area, which improves circulation. Softened by a neutral palette, the striking linear dimensions of the room are a focal point for the core of the plan. Upper-level bridges surround the vaulted space, which is defined by exposed beams and square columns. A steel and polished-chrome lighting fixture sets off a contemporary glass-block wall that fuses the dining area with the space behind it.

master spa | At the rim of the deck adjoining the master suite, a step-up spa offers a panorama of the sea and striking views of the sunset. The outdoor space cantilevers above a main-level loggia and a splendid winding staircase that leads to ground-level parking and walkways to the beach.

master bedroom | Situated at the edge of the Gulf of Mexico, the plan employs walls of glass to bring in views and natural light throughout the interior. The owners' retreat features sliding doors and curved windows that open the bedroom to the breathtaking beauty and waterfront breezes of its inviting locale. At the edge of the spa-style tub, a peninsular three-view fireplace warms the spaces surrounding it, including the sitting area, bedroom and bath.

Mariska | SATER EARLY YEARS

site plan |

Oriented toward the Gulf of Mexico at the rear perimeter, the house takes full advantage of the views with retreating glass walls, spacious bays and curved windows that absorb scenery and bring in plenty of natural light. The front of the home overlooks a beach garden, and a mid-level loggia offers a unique entry inside. At the center of the plan, the formal dining room opens to the main living area, which links to the outdoor zone. The upper level offers spacious sleeping quarters, including a splendid master retreat with a morning kitchen, deck and spa.

SIDE VIEW

site plan legend

1 ENTRY PORTICO
2 FOYER
3 GALLERY
4 STUDY
5 ELEVATOR
6 POWDER BATH
7 GUEST BEDROOM #1
8 GUEST BATH #1
9 DINING ROOM
10 HALL
11 WET BAR
12 KITCHEN
13 PANTRY
14 LIVING ROOM
15 FIREPLACE
16 BREAKFAST NOOK
17 COVERED PATIO
18 BRIDGE/GALLERY
19 LOFT
20 UTILITY ROOM
21 GUEST BEDROOM #2
22 GUEST BATH #2
23 MASTER BEDROOM
24 MASTER BATH
25 MASTER WARDROBE
26 WET BAR
27 DECK
28 SPA
29 MOTOR COURT

LOWER LEVEL:
TWO 1-CAR GARAGES
GAME ROOM
EXERCISE ROOM

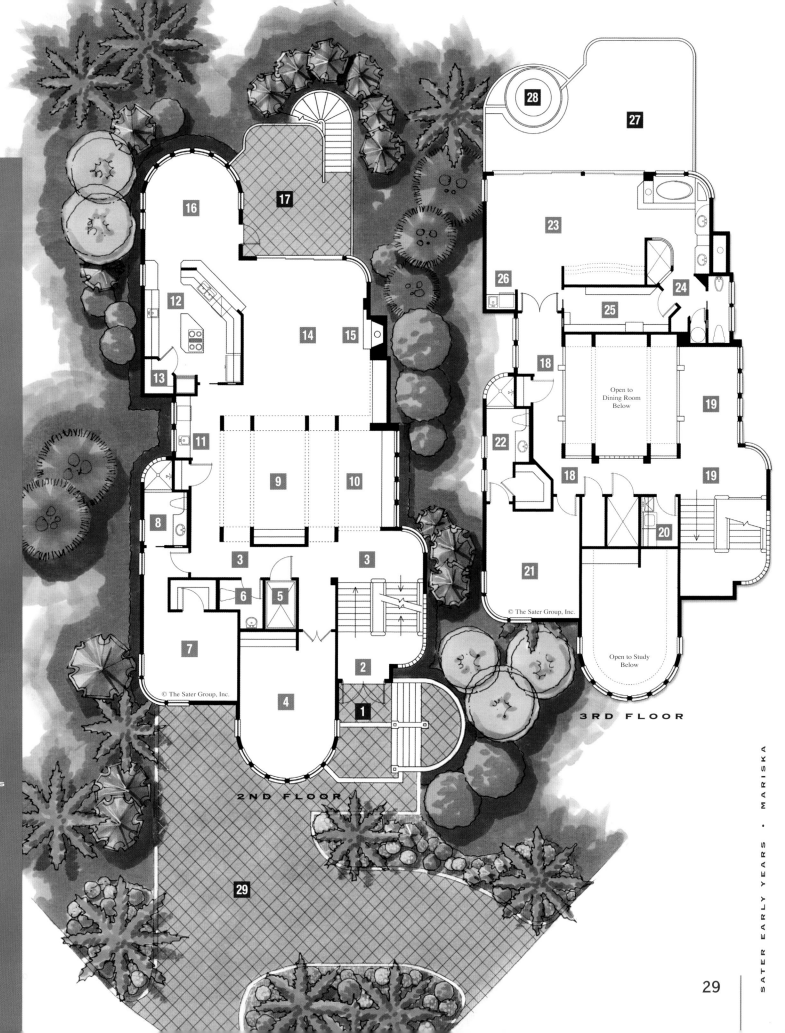

© The Sater Group, Inc.

2ND FLOOR

© The Sater Group, Inc.

3RD FLOOR

Alchemie

© THE SATER GROUP, INC.

Natural beauty surrounds a modern classic.

dan's notes | *The horizontal structure of this home achieves a careful balance with layered, asymmetrical gables and multifaceted rooms that add depth and texture to the elevation. My primary focus was on the relationship of the home to the landscape: the house is open to the south, facing the water, and the main living areas border a nearly continuous wall of glass. With roots in the Midwest, my clients wanted a clear link between the indigenous surroundings and the post-modern sensibility of the home, so I added regional brick accents and created an open, silo-style form for the dining room.*

Situated on a site that slopes toward a winding river, this prominent contemporary plan expresses a cultural association with its Midwestern setting through the use of regional materials, such as pale-brick panels and piers. Native fieldstone surrounds the lower walkout level and a wrapping lanai, without interfering with views of the woods and waterway. The long, semi-public southeastern face looks toward the river from all floors, addressing wide vistas with an open arrangement of rooms. Curved layers of glass illuminate the interior during daylight hours, and reflect delicately lit rooms at night. Structured to engage panoramas of scenery with highly functional rooms, the unique, tri-axial plan establishes intimate links with the site.

LOCATION: GREENVILLE, OHIO

BUILDER: DALE RISMILLER

LANDSCAPE ARCHITECT:
SMALLWOOD DESIGN GROUP,
SCOTT WINDHAM, ASLA

INTERIOR DESIGN: ROBB & STUCKY

PHOTOGRAPHY BY: BILL SWARTZ

rear exterior | Panels of earthen-hued brick create accents of texture and color between sweeping rows of stucco and glass at the rear elevation. Soaring roof forms energize the striking linear dimensions of the elevation, capped by a copper-topped chimney.

leisure room | A gable of windows grant wide river views to the leisure room and loft, set off by a very modern series of soaring floating arches, or buttresses, which repeat the forms of the rear elevation.

dining room | Built over a koi pond, the circular formal dining room evokes the simple form of a Midwest silo, taking in 360-degree views.

Alchemie | SATER EARLY YEARS

4 BEDROOM
5 FULL BATHS
2 HALF BATHS
12,247 SQ. FT.
LIVING AREA

front exterior | With a series of triangular forms on the entry and side gables, the forward façade offers a highly geometric profile to the streetscape. In striking contrast to the clean, contemporary theme of the elevation, a glass-enclosed turret harboring the dining room features a copper standing-seam roof—an historic reference that deepens the dimensions of the architecture.

site plan | Designed to take advantage of river views, the plan creates a multi-level wall of glass that infuses the interior with natural light and panoramas of scenery. At the front of the home, a sheltered bridge and portico lead across a koi pond and garden to the formal entry. An interior gallery connects the open stair hall and living room with the grand dining room—enclosed in a glass turret with views over the pond—and the casual living wing. The master suite includes a vaulted-glass sitting area and a bath with individual sweeping bays for the tub and shower. Upper-level guest suites cluster around a loft overlooking the leisure room.

34

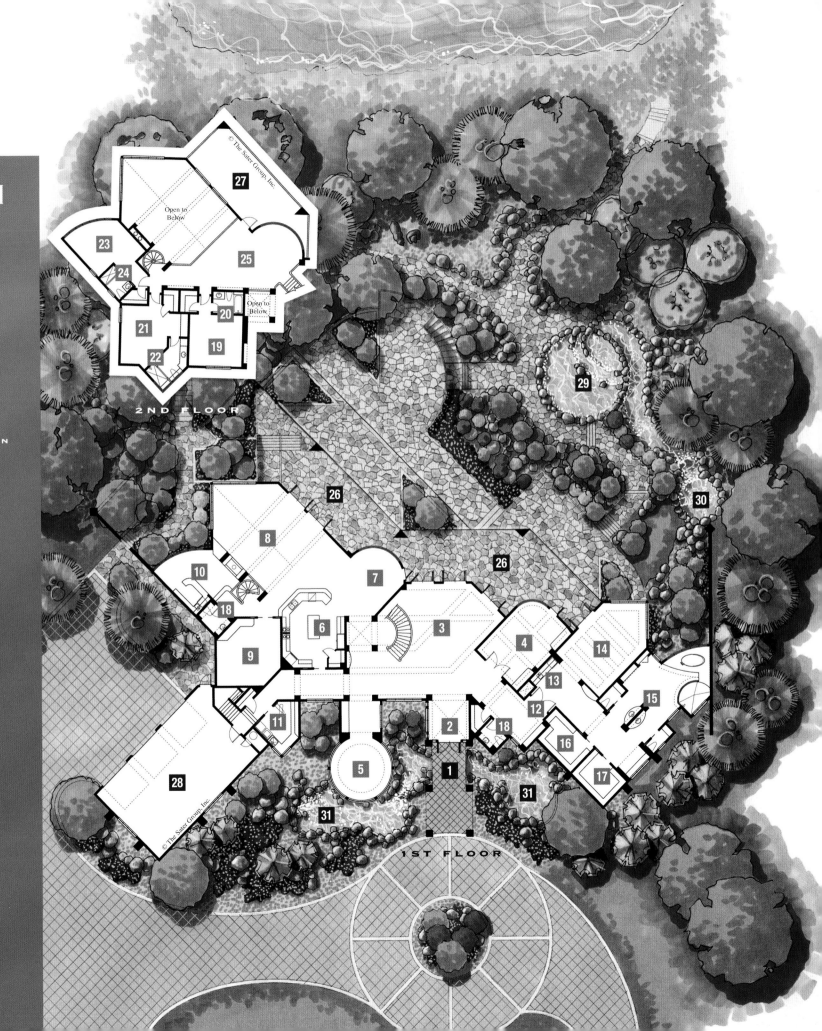

2ND FLOOR

1ST FLOOR

© The Sater Group, Inc.

90's

A BOLD NEW STYLE

The formative years

During the 1990s, The Sater Group continued to develop its unique brand of residential architecture, treating the demands of a mushrooming, trans-generational market with adventurous works designed for the subtropical climate of Florida. As the Sater client base grew, others elsewhere began to take notice as well, with the firm winning more than 250 national architectural awards in that decade alone. With further opportunity to experiment, Dan began to envision the application of his concepts involving the use of organic space to more traditional designs. Rather than recreate purely classical themes, Dan sculpted inventive derivatives in eclectic palettes with the passion of an impressionist artist. A growing list of clients found that these same concepts could be implemented in many other climates, and employed The Sater Group to create homes in diverse locations and in a variety of styles.

Dan also felt that his homes should be four-dimensional; that is, the exterior values should be reflected throughout the home's interior. Design elements unique to Sater houses found their way into highly detailed interiors with elaborately sculpted ceilings, reflective built-ins and thoughtfully designed fireplaces. Ceiling treatments could be used to define the function of the particular room it sheltered; for example, a living room may receive and impress guests, and so demands a more formal application than in a master suite, which is a more personal environment. Interior spaces in Dan's burgeoning portfolio became as exceptional as the designs they graced.

Outdoor living areas became even more of an event in Sater homes, with defined spaces such as solanas, conversational seating around fire pits, alfresco kitchens, dining rooms and even game rooms. Ceilings likewise defined and even modified those spaces, which became not merely appendages but rather thematic extensions of the home.

Over time, it became apparent that a Sater home was unique in a multitude of ways— not only in the casual elegance it exuded, its sculptural qualities or even its symbiotic relationship with the site, but rather the way the home seemed to take on a character of its own, with a singular purpose: to satisfy the lifestyle of its owners.

Windsor

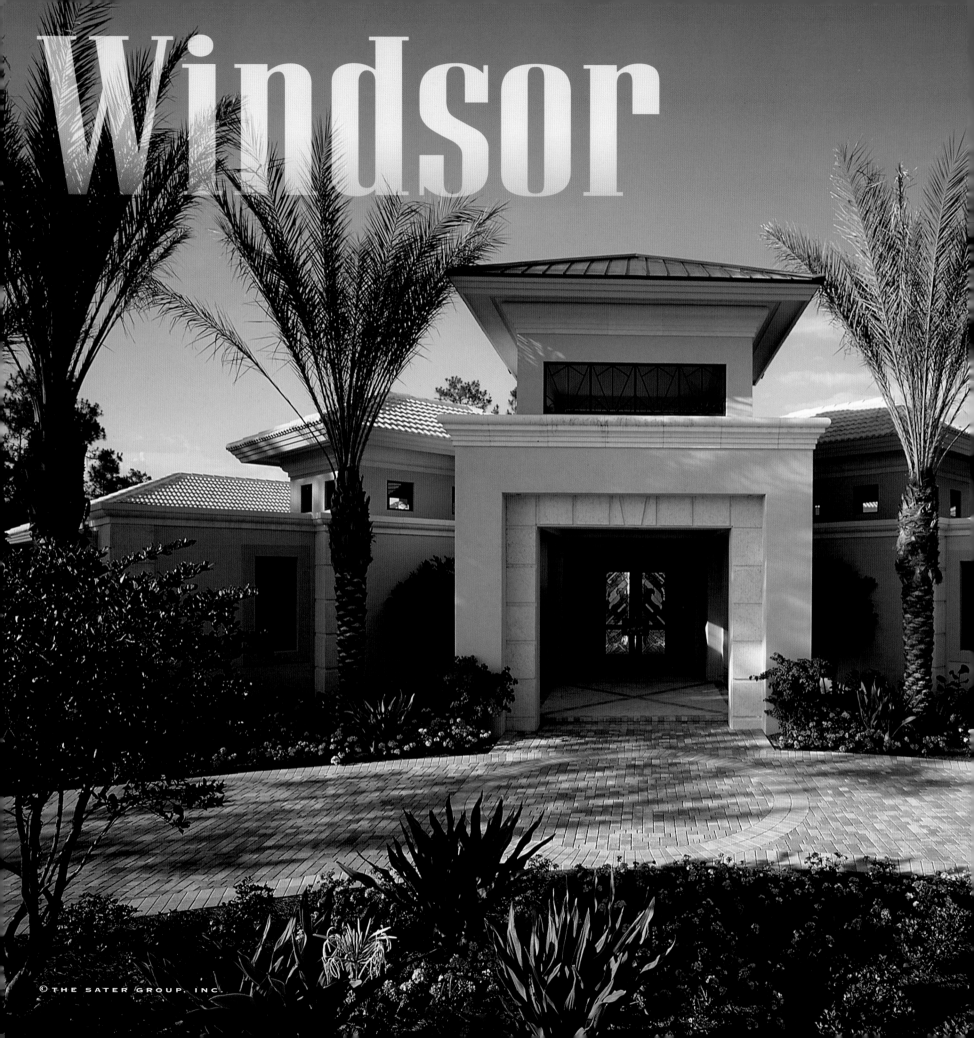

© THE SATER GROUP, INC.

Courtyard plan is wrapped by the sounds of water.

dan's notes | *This contemporary design was drawn to fit a complex landscape plan, including a large, man-made pond bordered with quarried rocks and limestone. Working with a careful interplay of water, softscapes and outside living spaces, I created a courtyard plan that would integrate the house with its site and breathe new life into traditional coastal dialects. The house breaks free of its skin in several places, such as the glass-encased study, which cantilevers above the main pool, and the gathering room, which juts out over the pond. It's a casual, comfortable home designed to connect intimately with the outdoors.*

Developed in the 1990s as a villa-style courtyard retreat, this golf course home took on the additional challenge of creating a water feature that would buffer the living spaces and offer excellent views. Interspersed with pools and ponds, the airy, open interior extends across the property, intimately linked with comfortable outdoor environments and spectacular views. Walls of glass and retreating doors offer fluid boundaries with verandas and decks, and mitered bays cantilever above bodies of water that enhance the scenery. The master suite wraps a secluded koi pond with a sitting retreat, sun decks, walkways and a garden bath with retractable walls.

LOCATION: NAPLES, FLORIDA

BUILDER: LIFESTYLE CONCEPTS, INC.

LANDSCAPE ARCHITECT:
SMALLWOOD DESIGN GROUP

INTERIOR DESIGN:
NAPLES DESIGN COLLECTION

PHOTOGRAPHY BY:
LAURENCE TAYLOR
& OSCAR THOMPSON

39

study | Set apart from the master suite, a glass-encased study cantilevers above the pool, lined by a walkway. A showcase of the designer's skill in interpreting mannerist influences, the bay exhibits classical and contemporary elements unified by linear forms. Flared rooflines create deep overhangs above the mitered window, while a square cupola evokes Italianate roots.

dining/living rooms | Open to the veranda at the back of the space, the informal living area is oriented toward the pond. An angled wet bar and mitered-glass panels extend above the water, lending spectacular views during daylight hours. Establishing a pattern of square arches, a massive propylaeum-style surround captures the eye and leads to the living room.

pool cabana | Secluded to the side property, the spa and shallow end of the pool face a rock garden and waterfall encased in greenery. Cabanas frame the space with sheltered sitting areas designed for contemplation. Wrought-iron gates lead to the outer zone, which winds back to the pond. Stucco pilasters feature a running entablature that follows the garden wall, wrapping the scenery with classic architecture.

master bedroom | Mitered windows frame the owners' bedroom, permitting views of the private outdoor living areas, which include a koi pond, sun deck and master garden. The central steps lead to a meditative retreat with a fireplace and access to the pool, spa and decks through French doors. A neutral palette unites the multi-level of the suite, and creates a deep sense of serenity.

Windsor | SATER 90'S

3 BEDROOM
3-1/2 BATH
6,457 SQ. FT.
LIVING AREA

site plan | Situated beside a crystal-clear pond created to enhance golf course views, the plan encompasses softscapes, pools and ponds that engage indoor spaces with a sense of nature. Casita-style guest suites frame the entry portico, providing a processional experience to the courtyard and veranda. Retreating glass doors form a fluid boundary with the gathering room—an angled space that stretches over the water— and visually links the front and rear properties. The foyer leads to a unique arrangement of the formal rooms, with the dining room jutting onto the veranda. A rambling master retreat links intimately with the landscape, with doors leading out to a private sun deck, pool and spa. Retractable walls frame the owners' bath, creating an outdoor garden environment inside the home.

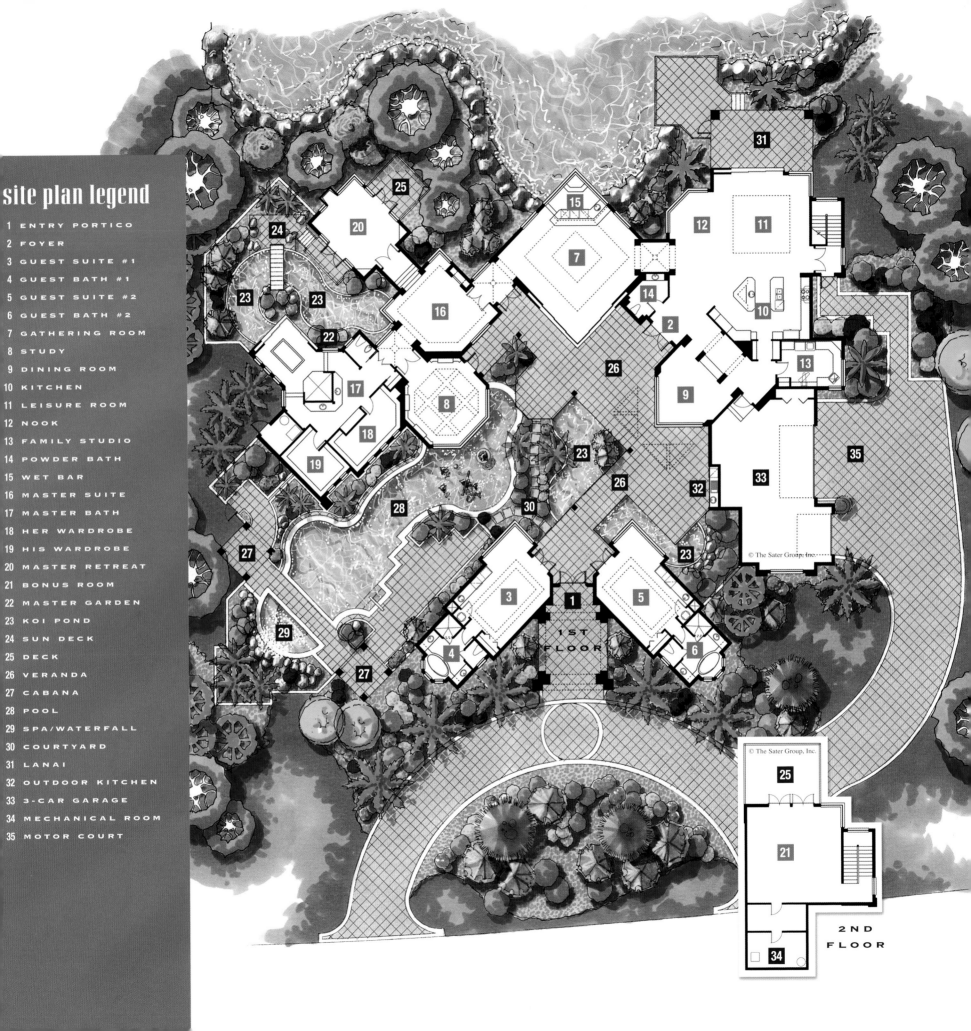

site plan legend

1 ENTRY PORTICO
2 FOYER
3 GUEST SUITE #1
4 GUEST BATH #1
5 GUEST SUITE #2
6 GUEST BATH #2
7 GATHERING ROOM
8 STUDY
9 DINING ROOM
10 KITCHEN
11 LEISURE ROOM
12 NOOK
13 FAMILY STUDIO
14 POWDER BATH
15 WET BAR
16 MASTER SUITE
17 MASTER BATH
18 HER WARDROBE
19 HIS WARDROBE
20 MASTER RETREAT
21 BONUS ROOM
22 MASTER GARDEN
23 KOI POND
24 SUN DECK
25 DECK
26 VERANDA
27 CABANA
28 POOL
29 SPA/WATERFALL
30 COURTYARD
31 LANAI
32 OUTDOOR KITCHEN
33 3-CAR GARAGE
34 MECHANICAL ROOM
35 MOTOR COURT

1ST FLOOR

© The Sater Group, Inc.

2ND FLOOR

Milano

© THE SATER GROUP, INC.

Island villa captures breathtaking views.

dan's notes | *In the mid-1990s, country-western singer Alan Jackson asked me to design a recreational getaway in a tropical environment that he and his family could use for boating and fishing. I envisioned a view-oriented series of rooms—each with its own connection to the outdoors—and a walkway that leads from the lanai to the dock on the bay. I came up with the idea of extending large expanses of glass toward the water, and opening the core of the home to the outside. A curved tower is suspended above the main pool, which runs the length of the rear perimeter. Contemporary lines are integrated with elements of the past, such as a classic colonnade and a clay-tile roof.*

An idyllic setting for a remote waterside residence, beautiful Marco Island harbors this contemporary Mediterranean retreat—originally designed as a custom pied-à-terre for superstar Alan Jackson—an award-winning plan deemed by some observers to be one of America's finest homes. Far from the bustle of the city, the waterfront villa faces the Gulf of Mexico—several hundred yards away—with lengthy frontage to the east along Collier Bay. Unspoiled scenery and stunning views dominate each room, and walls seem a mere formality in an elegant home that links so easily to the outside. An expansive lanai unifies the plan, linking the public and informal rooms with inviting *plein air* spaces.

LOCATION: MARCO ISLAND, FLORIDA

BUILDER: SLOCUM CHRISTIAN

LANDSCAPE ARCHITECT:
SMALLWOOD DESIGN GROUP,
SCOTT WINDHAM, ASLA

INTERIOR DESIGN:
MARC MICHAELS INTERIORS

PHOTOGRAPHY BY:
LAURENCE TAYLOR

SATER 90'S · MILANO

rear view | Classic elements come together with carved contemporary forms along the rear elevation, where a mitered-glass turret harboring the morning nook and upper-level library/loft cantilevers above the pool. Angled corner transoms define the interior space above the retractable glass doors of the living room, which overlooks the lanai and Collier Bay. A grand double portico mimics the varied pattern of forms along the elevation, and a rooftop deck balances the rhythm with a series of simple balustrades.

rear view twilight | The lower lanai wraps the pool arena, repeating the sinuous curves of the turret and providing overlooks to the water. Suspended over the pool, the loft and lower-level nook offer a highly sculpted form that projects beyond the home's perimeter and provides an 180-degree view that takes in glimpses of the horizon. An outdoor kitchen near the retreating doors of the leisure room leads to the veranda, while the upper portico offers an observation deck that is accessible from the media room and loft.

living room |
Arched transoms suspended at a 90-degree angle offer a seamless boundary to the outdoors in the central living room. Soaring ceilings subdued only by the scenery enhance a sense of openness that prevails throughout the home. Varied elements—the striking lines of the coffered ceiling, the angled transoms and the curve of the glass—create a unique architectural statement that wraps the room in warmth and a sense of intimacy.

veranda |
Walls surrounding the living room retreat to sixteen feet on each side, bringing in a breathtaking panorama of Collier Bay. In harmony with the elements and subject to the whims of sun and shade, the interior space employs a palette of materials suited to the Southeastern climate. Interior spaces relate easily to the outdoors yet protect the privacy of the owners.

Milano | SATER 90'S

leisure room/kitchen | Designed for informal entertaining, the leisure room adjoins the kitchen and snack counter and leads to an outdoor dining area. Graceful arches ease the transition to the living and dining rooms via a vestibule with access to the lanai.

site plan | Designed to fit the wedge-shaped lot, the entire house is engaged with the outdoors, wrapped by a lanai that extends the living spaces and leads to the 350-foot frontage on Collier Bay. Mitered-glass breakfast and loft areas, as well as retreating doors in the leisure and living rooms, permit sweeping views of the water and open the home to the outside. An elaborate master suite features a morning kitchen, private terrace, an exercise room and a study, while a guest house enjoys a private lanai. An upper-level media room leads to the observation deck, and hidden stairs provide access to a wide rooftop deck.

SATER 90'S · MILANO

site plan legend

1 ENTRY
2 FOYER
3 STUDY
4 DINING ROOM
5 HER BATH
6 HIS BATH
7 MASTER SUITE
8 HER WARDROBE
9 HIS WARDROBE
10 MORNING KITCHEN
11 EXERCISE
12 MASTER FOYER
13 MASTER GARDEN
14 POOL BATH
15 BREAKFAST NOOK
16 KITCHEN
17 LEISURE ROOM
18 FIREPLACE
19 LIVING ROOM
20 GUEST SUITE
21 GUEST BATH
22 OUTDOOR KITCHEN
23 LANAI
24 POOL
25 OBSERVATION DECK
26 MECHANICAL ROOM
27 UTILITY ROOM
28 MEDIA ROOM
29 BEDROOM #1
30 BATH #1
31 BEDROOM #2
32 BATH #2
33 BEDROOM #3
34 BATH #3
35 LOFT
36 LOFT/LIBRARY
37 STAIRS TO ROOF
38 3-CAR GARAGE
39 PORTE-COCHERE
40 SPA

1ST FLOOR

© The Sater Group, Inc.

Open to Below

Open to Below

Open to Below

Open to Below

Flat Deck

© The Sater Group, Inc.

2ND FLOOR

McKenna

© THE SATER GROUP, INC.

Contemporary classic embraces wide views of the river.

dan's notes | *This waterfront plan requires open space with exposure to views and access to outdoor living areas, so I designed the house around the landscape, oriented toward the river with panels of glass to take in the scenery. The home captures a sense of the region in unique ways, with a complex elevation that adds depth and textural interest to the contemporary European styling. I wanted the core of the home—the central living area—to be entirely open, from the entry to the steps leading down to the pool, with outstanding views and a subtle sense of tradition.*

On the banks of the Imperial River, in Bonita Springs, this modern Mediterranean villa boasts a subdued contemporary elevation and a deeply comfortable floor plan. The core of the home opens to a winding terrace and a sculpted pool and spa area that overlooks the river. Retreating glass doors create seamless boundaries that take in scenery and allow fresh air to circulate throughout the interior. To the left of the entry, a rotunda and dome ceiling illuminate the circular stairwell leading to the lofts and recreation areas. On the upper level, a media room and secluded office complement the private master retreat on the main floor. To the right of the plan, guest quarters, a game room and deck share a loft, and an exercise room leads to a remote suite above the garage.

LOCATION:
BONITA SPRINGS, FLORIDA

BUILDER: LIFESTYLE CONCEPTS, INC.

LANDSCAPE ARCHITECT:
W. CHRISTIAN BUSK, ASLA

INTERIOR DESIGN:
ACCESSORIES ETC., INC.
CHRISSIE FORBES, ASID

PHOTOGRAPHY BY:
LAURENCE TAYLOR

SATER 90'S • MCKENNA

MCKENNA

rear deck | Like the bow of a ship, the grand central gable extends toward the outdoor retreat, defining the rear perimeter and connecting the interior with a sense of nature. Bays harboring a cabana, formal dining room, and a guest suite open to the pool and spa area, which overlooks the Imperial River.

living room/entry | The rear wall of the living room opens completely to the outside, creating a seamless boundary with the terrace and pool arena. Open from the entry through the core of the home, the living room engages the senses with views of the outdoors and vistas carried by sight lines and the dramatic curves of the architecture. A series of transoms amplifies the home's dialogue with the environment and offers a pronounced view of the entry from the outside.

57

McKenna | SATER 90'S

4 BEDROOM
4 FULL BATH
3 HALF BATH
7,852 SQ. FT.
LIVING AREA

living room | Soaring ceiling forms and a dramatic rotunda hover above the stairs near the open foyer and living room. A sweeping balustrade visually anchors the entry space, and leads to a loft overlooking the main level. Stone floors unify the living area with the terrace, which leads to the pool and spa.

site plan | A porte-cochere leads to a central motor court, and the formal entry of the home, and to a side entrance that links to the kitchen. The grand foyer opens to the main living area and terrace, creating a natural synchronicity with the outdoors. Surrounded by mitered-glass windows and retreating glass walls, the stunning pool arena overlooks views of the Imperial River. Remote bays harboring a private cabana, office and guest suite offer extraordinary vistas, and outer steps lead to the river dock.

site plan legend

1 ENTRY
2 GRAND FOYER
3 LIVING ROOM
4 MASTER SUITE
5 MASTER CABANA
6 MASTER BATH
7 HIS/HER WARDROBE
8 POWDER BATH
9 KITCHEN
10 DINING ROOM
11 LEISURE ROOM
12 WET BAR
13 UTILITY ROOM
14 BUTLER'S PANTRY
15 GUEST SUITE
16 POOL BATH
17 BEDROOM #1
18 BEDROOM BATH #1
19 LOFT
20 GAME ROOM
21 BEDROOM #2
22 BEDROOM BATH #2
23 COVERED WALKWAY
24 LIBRARY/LOFT
25 MEDIA ROOM
26 MEDIA ROOM BATH
27 OFFICE
28 EXERCISE ROOM
29 EXERCISE BATH
30 GUEST DECK
31 1-1/2-CAR GARAGE
32 2-CAR GARAGE
33 VERANDA
34 POOL
35 SPA
36 MASTER SUN DECK
37 MOTOR COURT
38 OUTDOOR KITCHEN
39 DOCK

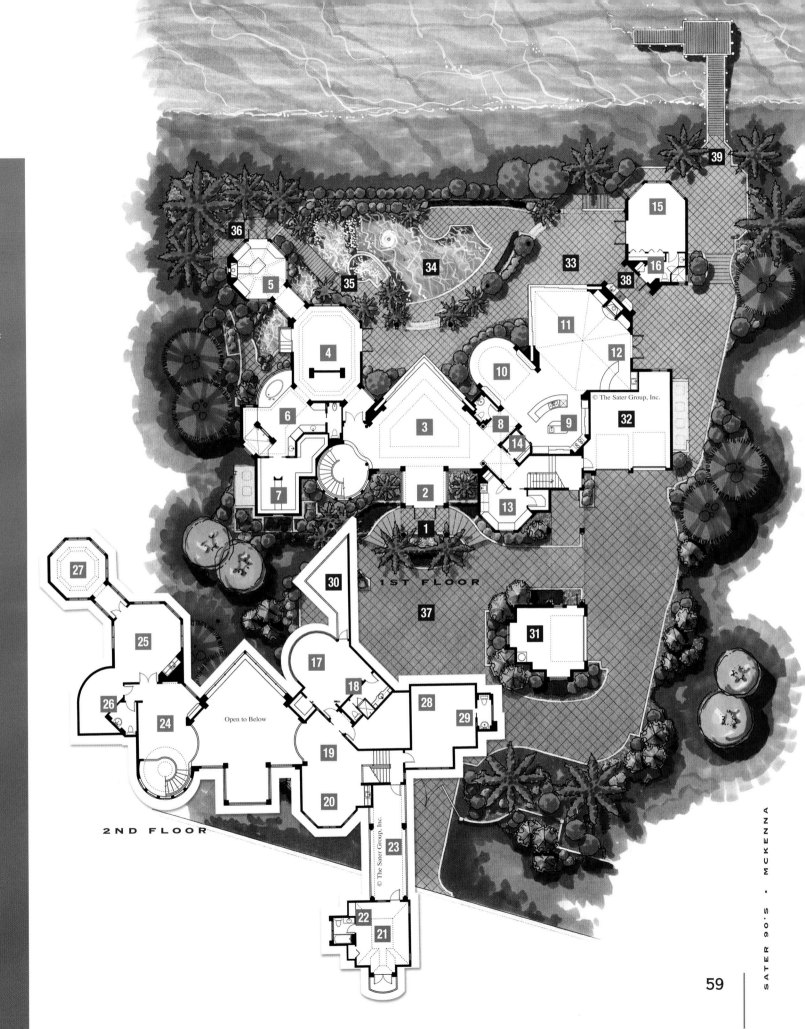

SATER 90'S • MCKENNA

Sumatra

© THE SATER GROUP, INC.

Smart waterfront home lives well inside and out.

dan's notes | *One of my favorite houses is this European-style villa designed for an exceptional couple whose schedules, I know, are jam-packed. Bill and Lynda Steere wanted a place on the water—not too grand, with views to the front and back of the plan. The owners entertain frequently yet informally, so I designed the kitchen and dining room to work together to accommodate crowds and caterers, as well as everyday meals for two. Open interior spaces and easy transitions to the outdoors were primary considerations, and the close relationship between the library and the central veranda is a vital element in the home's circulation.*

This contemporary Mediterranean-style home enjoys panoramas of the Imperial River, just off the Gulf of Mexico. Sited at a bend in the river, the home employs its unique position on the peninsula to integrate views with a variety of interior and outside spaces.

An angled entry opens to the gallery-style foyer with views that extend through the core of the home. The library functions as a traditional space for guests, with a loft that increases the visual dimensions of the room. To the right of the entrance hall, the casual living zone integrates flexible gathering spaces with a highly organized culinary area. The adjacent dining room serves as a casual nook as well as a place for guests to mingle.

Upstairs, a private wing harbors a work place and study, with a deck overlooking the river. A bridge connects the office to a loft and library, as well as an exercise room.

LOCATION:
BONITA SPRINGS, FLORIDA

BUILDER:
CRONACHER DEVELOPMENT CORP.

LANDSCAPE ARCHITECT:
W. CHRISTIAN BUSK, ASLA

INTERIOR DESIGN:
ACCESSORIES ETC., INC.
CHRISSIE FORBES, ASID

PHOTOGRAPHY BY:
LAURENCE TAYLOR

library | Open to the foyer, the library functions
as a formal room on traditional occasions, yet is
undeniably in harmony with the elements, linked to
a forward balcony via a trio of French doors. At the
foreground, a plush wicker sofa, stacked with hand-
embroidered cushions collected by the owners in
Indonesia, marks the boundary from the interior to the
veranda. The space grants extensive vistas in both direc-
tions, with views of an inlet—named "The Fishbowl" by
locals—toward the front property, and fine panoramas
of the Imperial River across the rear perimeter.

library/loft | A loft and overlook wrap the library,
enhancing the spatial dimensions of the room and
lending a sense of texture to the central living area.
Square transoms and a wall of glass fit the room with
a sense of the outdoors and permit vistas of the pool,
spa and rear property. Beyond the retreating doors,
a massive stone fireplace framed by custom lighting
fixtures enriches the seating area of the veranda.

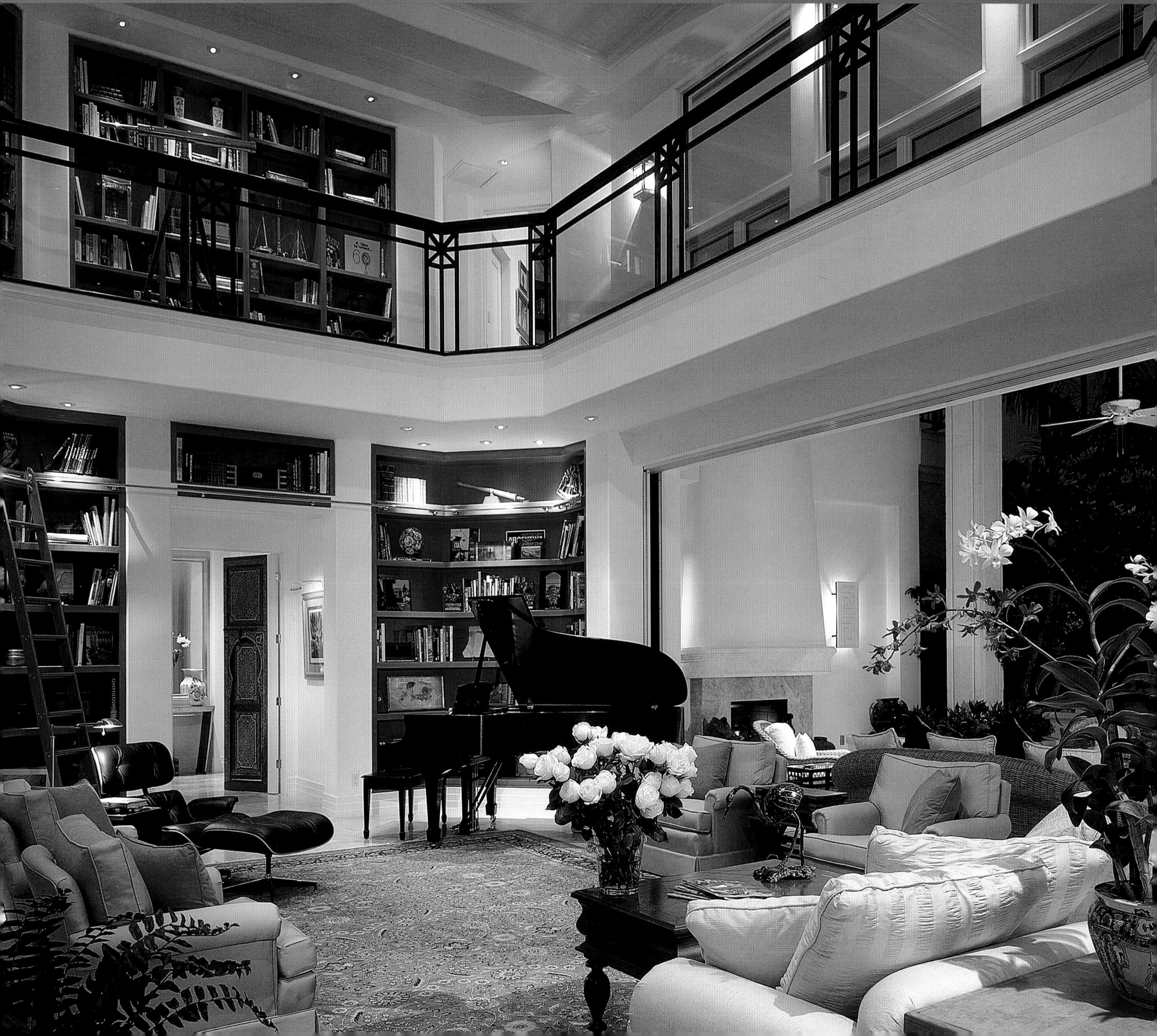

dining and family rooms | To the right of the foyer, a bar sink and serving counter facilitate planned events in the formal dining room—an open arena with splendid river views—which flexes to casual space for family meals. Stone floors unify the public and private realms, with a neutral palette that expresses the relaxed theme of the house. Carved ceiling coves and coffers help to define the individual functions of the rooms and accentuate the sculptural qualities of the design. Elegant dining fauteuils are counterbalanced by deeply comfortable, pale-leather furnishings framing the media wall in the leisure room.

kitchen | A splendid bay window brightens the rear wall of the kitchen, which is equipped for crowd-size gatherings as well as impromptu events. Marble countertops and anigre cabinetry conceal up-to-the-minute appliances and lend a sense of texture to the culinary décor. A seating niche at the morning counter is designed for daily meals, and flexes as a serving area for planned events. Above the food-preparation counter, dual lighting fixtures—ship lights recovered from a London vessel shop—express a nautical theme that appears throughout the home.

dining room | Views of the veranda wrap the rear perimeter of the formal dining room through a mitered-glass window, which provides plenty of daylight during morning meals. A sculpted niche harbors a built-in contemporary sideboard of maple and midnight-black marble, enhanced with fine collectibles from the owners' travels. The print of Canvass Back Ducks, from an original watercolor by John James Audubon, was a gift to the owner by his father, William Campbell Steere.

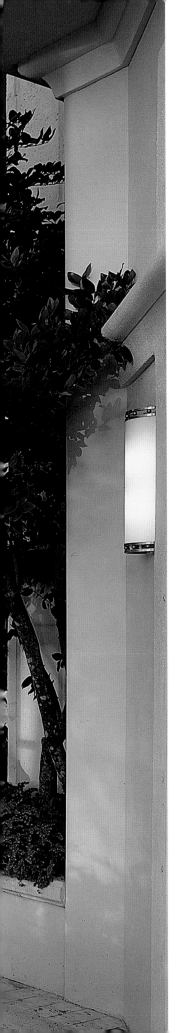

veranda | Conversation seating surrounds a massive stone fireplace on the veranda—an outside space intimately linked with the interior living area—less than a stone's throw from the steps leading into the pool and spa. Twin backlit ceramic panels accentuated by an Art Deco theme lend a subtle enhancement to the outdoor living space. Cloud-white cushions and wicker frames maintain the theme of elegant comfort, which prevails throughout the home. Rough-honed stone floors unify the outdoor spaces with the interior, where a polished version of the stone is used.

rear pool view | A wrapping veranda offers a central sitting area near the pool and fountain. The deck above the leisure room is accessed by the guest suite and exercise room on the upper level, where a loft and overlook expand the dimensions of the interior. On the main level, glass doors retreat to dissolve the boundary between the leisure room and the outer retreat. To the left, an outdoor kitchen and alfresco dining area accommodates even formal occasions.

Sumatra | SATER 90'S

front/side exterior | A series of elegant arches framed by bay turrets lines the side of the home, to the left of the formal entry, enhancing a Mediterranean scheme of cream-white stucco and clay-tile roofs. Subtropical greenery surrounds the façade, which is oriented in two directions, toward the bay and the Imperial River.

site plan | An angled entry leads from a terraced exterior staircase to the grand foyer, which offers vistas to both the front and rear of the home—where the river winds from an inlet (The Fishbowl) toward the bay. The library serves as the formal center of the plan, wrapped by a loft overlook and built-in cabinets. Retractable doors meld the interior space with an outdoor retreat. To the right of the plan,

the dining room and kitchen facilitate planned gatherings as well as everyday life, with flexible serving counters and food-prep areas that are spacious enough for five-star caterers. The master wing features a gallery which separates the shared spaces from a private retreat with a bay window. Upstairs, a secluded study links via an overlook to the exercise room and two guest suites.

site plan legend

1 ENTRY
2 FOYER
3 KITCHEN
4 DINING
5 LEISURE ROOM
6 LIBRARY
7 MASTER SUITE
8 MASTER BATH
9 HER WARDROBE
10 HIS WARDROBE
11 POWDER BATH
12 STUDY
13 STUDY BATH
14 GUEST SUITE #1
15 GUEST BATH #1
16 GUEST SUITE #2
17 GUEST BATH #2
18 EXERCISE ROOM
19 LOFT/LIBRARY
20 OVERLOOK
21 DECK
22 POOL BATH
23 ELEVATOR
24 OUTDOOR KITCHEN
25 VERANDA
26 POOL
27 FOUNTAIN
28 LAUNDRY
29 OUTDOOR FIREPLACE
30 DOCK

LOWER LEVEL:
3-CAR GARAGE
PUTTING GREEN
STORAGE

© The Sater Group, Inc.

1ST FLOOR

© The Sater Group, Inc.

2ND FLOOR

Valli

© THE SATER GROUP, INC.

Riverfront manor pays tribute to modern architecture.

dan's notes | *This is an adventurous work with many modern components as well as an amalgam of fundamental, organic components. The site wraps a bend in the waterway and, naturally, the clients wanted plenty of views, so I designed the forward core of the plan to overlook the southern lagoon and oriented the rear perimeter toward the river. The dramatic glass gable makes a statement about the contemporary nature of the home, yet the rooms are designed to flow easily from one space to another: it's a very livable home.*

Slightly below a bend in the Imperial River, the site also overlooks an islet of the Fishbowl bayou—named for its unusual shape—and, to the west, the Gulf of Mexico. Angled lines define the contemporary elevation, which wraps the waterway and offers panoramic views across the rear perimeter. The formal core of the home overlooks the koi pond, pool and spa, while an interior breezeway opens to a vaulted formal dining room with a "floating" beam ceiling and walls of glass that fill the space with natural light. Public rooms progress seamlessly into the private wings of the home, while a gallery segues into the master foyer, providing pocket-door access to the owners' exercise room. Ceiling coves and coffers offer definition to airy rooms that flex to facilitate many functions. Throughout the home, a pleasing juxtaposition of modern aesthetics and traditional flow creates a natural environment and a sense of elegance.

LOCATION:
BONITA SPRINGS, FLORIDA

BUILDER: LIFESTYLE CONCEPTS, INC.

LANDSCAPE ARCHITECT:
W. CHRISTIAN BUSK, ASLA

INTERIOR DESIGN:
LISA LOVETTO

PHOTOGRAPHY BY:
LAURENCE TAYLOR

leisure room | A lighted cove ceiling engages
the informal living area with subtle illumination and
enriches the texture of the area. Open to the kitchen
and nook, the leisure room is adjacent to a snack
counter that easily serves impromptu meals and
gatherings. The octagonal shape of the room permits
panoramas of scenery through a series of tall
windows and opens to the outdoors via mitered walls
that align with the geometry of the space. A stone-
tile TV surround serves as a focal point, framed by
paneled shelves.

inside rear view | Floating boxed beams
create a sense of drama and align views of an inland
waterway and islet through the vaulted wall of glass
above the formal dining room. Parallel to the formal
entry, large mitered windows extend toward the front
property with an openness that looks beyond the
boundaries of the space.

Valli | SATER 90'S

site plan legend

1 ENTRY
2 FOYER
3 DINING ROOM
4 MASTER SUITE
5 MASTER BATH
6 MASTER CLOSET
7 EXERCISE ROOM
8 UTILITY ROOM
9 LIVING ROOM
10 BREEZEWAY
11 KITCHEN
12 NOOK
13 LEISURE ROOM
14 POWDER BATH
15 GUEST SUITE #1
16 GUEST BATH #1
17 GUEST SUITE #2
18 GUEST BATH #2
19 GUEST SUITE #3
20 GUEST BATH #3
21 MEDIA ROOM
22 GAME ROOM
23 STUDY
24 BATHROOM #4
25 BAR
26 CATWALK
27 STORAGE
28 OUTDOOR KITCHEN
29 LANAI
30 DECK
31 POOL
32 SPA
33 WATER FEATURE
34 3-CAR GARAGE
35 SUN DECK
36 DOCK
37 MOTOR COURT

rear exterior | Broad steps lead to the wrapping lanai above the lush pool and spa, which surrounds the rear perimeter and adjoins a koi pond edging the formal living room. Water features on this side of the elevation present an illusion of a stream that runs through the core of the home.

dining room | A breezeway connecting the living room and foyer to the casual wing overlooks the formal dining room, with views to the front property.

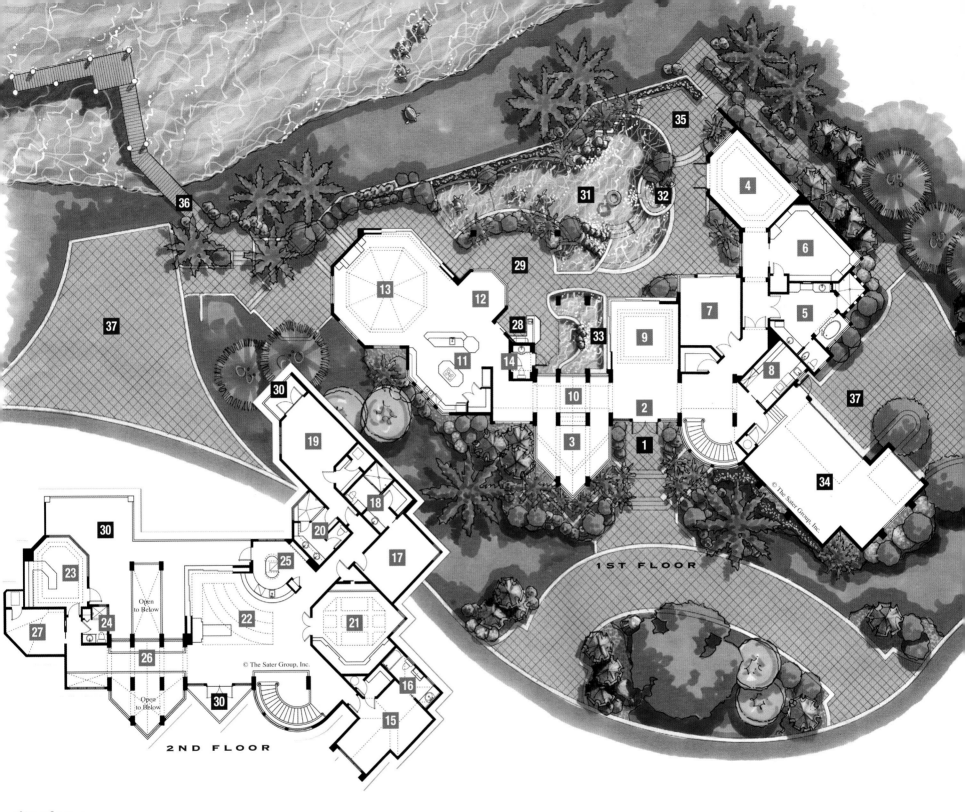

1ST FLOOR

2ND FLOOR

© The Sater Group, Inc.

© The Sater Group, Inc.

site plan | The dramatic glass-and-stucco façade makes a bold statement at the streetscape. Double entry doors lead to a grand reception hall linking the living spaces with a splendid master wing, which includes a spacious exercise room. Views extend in two directions toward the river—which bends at the site—and a wrapping lanai offers ample poolside seating and an outdoor kitchen. A glass turret harbors a winding staircase connecting the main-level gallery with a loft, recreation space and media room, flanked by two guest suites. To the right of the plan, a catwalk links to a private study with deck access and wide views of the river.

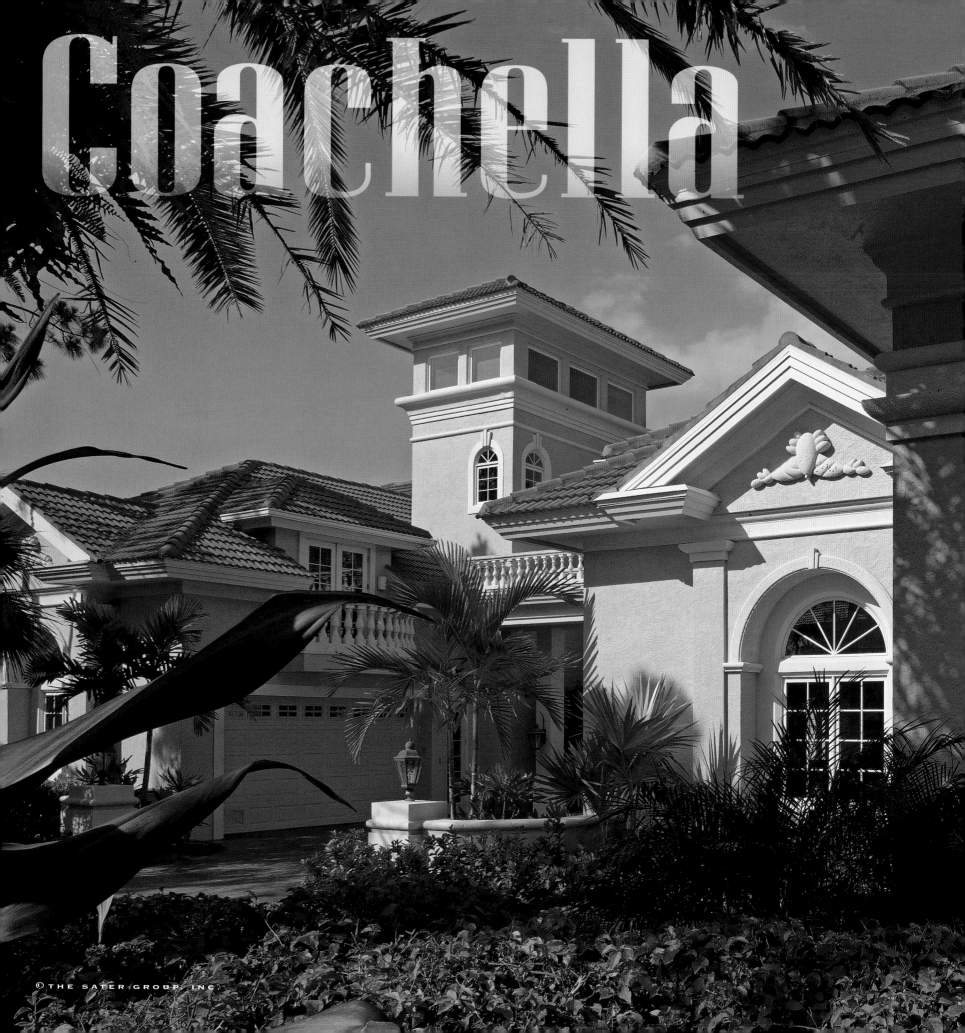

Coachella

© THE SATER GROUP, INC.

A captivating villa takes in bird's-eye views.

dan's notes | *There's a sense of grandeur about this retreat that goes beyond the European-style structure of the home. We started with an incredibly unique lot surrounded by water with an adjacent, smaller peninsula—where the guest casita is now located— and oriented the house toward the bay. There needed to be plenty of outside living spaces, so I drew the plan to follow the contours of the site and extended the veranda to encompass an outdoor dining area. The courtyard arcade offers a welcoming experience at the front of the home, and a variety of spaces unfold from the gallery.*

Surrounded by water, the house takes advantage of panoramic views with a series of bays, French doors and windows. A seasonal pied-à-terre, the primarily Italian-style villa promotes a sense of privacy through a gated entry and a stunning porte-cochere. Anchored by a sculpted fountain and lush planters, the forecourt leads to the formal entry and foyer via a processional experience that enhances the European flavor of the façade. The traditional rooms at the front of the plan open to the rear veranda, an arrangement that satisfies the clients' desire to entertain. A gallery hall and stairwell link the casual living zone to a mid-level guest suite and a private loft retreat at the top of the tower, which grants breathtaking views of the region. On the opposite side, a rambling master suite takes in bay vistas and provides its own access to the veranda and pool.

LOCATION:
BONITA SPRINGS, FLORIDA

BUILDER: PORTOFINO HOMES

LANDSCAPE ARCHITECT:
DENNIS CHURCH, ASLA
WILSON MILLER & ASSOC.

INTERIOR DESIGNER:
WANDA NELSON
DECORATING PREFERENCE

PHOTOGRAPHY BY: CJ WALKER

77

front entry | An inviting forecourt suggests the modern European theme that prevails throughout the home. Pavers mark a path to the Palladian-style entry in a progressive approach that encompasses a lush landscape tailored to the bayside locale. A low-relief carving above the central portico lends a sense of grace and warmth to the elevation. Neo-classical grillwork on a row of transom windows suggests a Palladian influence, and a fanlight above the paneled entry doors presents a glimpse of the past. Stunning bays frame the central entry, underscoring the symmetry of the design.

family room/veranda |

Retracting walls create a seamless transition to the outdoors at the rear perimeter, where the leisure room merges with the casual eating area of the veranda. Exposed cruciform beams add a sense of shelter to the family's living space, and enhance the visual dimensions of the room. Butternut cabinetry in the kitchen complements a deeply carved fireplace surround and wood-paneled media center.

breakfast nook | Open to the kitchen and leisure room, the breakfast nook takes in wide views of the veranda through a mitered-glass bay window, oriented to the pool and spa. A coffered ceiling highlights the room and echoes the arched forms of the colonnade that shelters the outside sitting area. Terra-hued walls surround the intimate casual dining room, set off by a vintage alabaster chandelier.

entry foyer | Both rustic and grand, the splendid entry foyer opens on both sides to the outdoors. Arched entries lead to the main gallery and dining room just beyond. Mosaic tiles—inlaid on a stone floor honed to reflect the muted finish of the walls and barrel-vaulted ceiling—mark the path of the gallery leading to the rear veranda.

kitchen | Seashell-colored granite counters surround the food-preparation area of the kitchen, providing a place for easy meals and impromptu family gatherings. Sleek appliances contrast with hand-painted tiles, which serve as a backsplash above the cooktop.

entry court | A sculpture of a young beachcomber flaunting a fiddler crab greets guests at the forecourt, just beyond the porte-cochere and entry gate.

dining room | The symmetry of the design is evident in the formal dining room, which features dual French doors to the veranda, framed by twin windows.

Coachella | SATER 90's

rear exterior | Keystone arches and piers with mid-level cornices enrich the colonnade bordering the veranda, which leads down broad steps to the pool and spa. The breakfast nook and leisure room enjoy views of the outside sitting and dining areas through the graceful forms of the arcade.

site plan | Sited on a peninsula, the plan employs a series of windows and wide panels of glass to engage the entire interior with water views. A porte-cochere, entry gate and forecourt offer a progressive approach to the front of the home. The foyer leads to a gallery connecting the public and private wings, and directly to the rear veranda.

Clustered around the kitchen, the breakfast nook and casual living space lead to the veranda via retreating doors. Beyond an outdoor kitchen, an alfresco dining area and veranda link to a secluded guest casita located on a corner of the peninsula. A three-story tower serves as a hub of circulation granting spectacular 360-degree views.

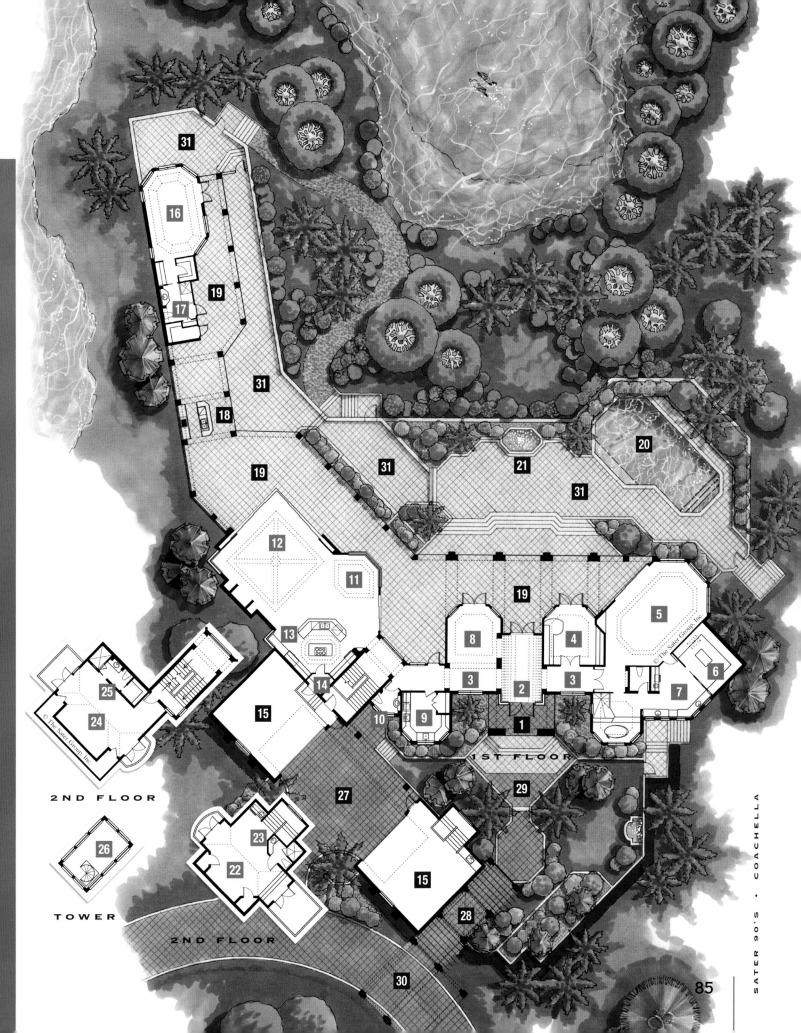

2ND FLOOR

TOWER

2ND FLOOR

1ST FLOOR

Mirada

© THE SATER GROUP, INC.

Avant-garde villa combines comfort and world-class style.

dan's notes | *In many ways, this is a revival home, with neoclassical lines and an interplay of contemporary elements, such as the stacked turrets and cantilevered bays. Primarily, the house conforms naturally to the site and responds to the region by incorporating light and views with a diversity of forms. My clients wanted a well-scaled, comfortable home, yet the abstract aspects of the design appealed to them as well. The house is literate in its approach to the past, with a bow to mid-century modern and international styles, but the overall sense of the home is one of spacious comfort and livability.*

A contemporary translation of ancient courtyard themes, this modern villa surrounds a veranda and koi pond that meander through the core of the design, connecting the rooms with an intimate sense of the outdoors. The internal circulation is enriched by a series of French doors and retreating glass walls that frame secluded views of the landscape. A pair of casitas frames the grand portico and colonnade that lead to a formal entry of serenely simple paneled-glass doors and sidelights. The dramatic roofline rising above the forecourt establishes the avant-garde theme, which prevails throughout the public and private realms—even to the idiosyncratic décor of the traditional spaces. This home is a pleasing mixture of modern and classic architecture, where well-carved fasciae and cornices enrich bays topped with transoms on cupolas.

LOCATION: NAPLES, FLORIDA

BUILDER:
BORAN CRAIG BARBER HOMES

LANDSCAPE ARCHITECT:
SMALLWOOD DESIGN GROUP

INTERIOR DESIGN:
URBAN STUDIO ASSOCIATES

PHOTOGRAPHY BY: CJ WALKER

dining room | A bow window grants a greater sense of space and light in the dining room, where views extend across the pool and spa to the fairway. An upholstered ceiling sports a galaxy of pinlights that shine down upon a sculpted table and hand-sewn leather chairs. The room was extended in size to create a practical space that would accommodate the owners' planned events.

kitchen | Sunshine-yellow lacquered cabinetry lines a sleek, contemporary kitchen designed for serious cooks. Polished terrazzo countertops unify the space, and a central dual-level island makes a high-impact statement with a stainless-steel frame and a row of retro swirl-patterned counter stools. A walk-in cooler and freezer, a separate wine room and convenient access to the outdoor kitchen enhance the function of this culinary space.

Mirada | SATER 90'S

7 BEDROOM
9-1/2 BATH
21,934 SQ. FT.
LIVING AREA

site plan legend

1 ENTRY
2 FOYER
3 GALLERY
4 POWDER BATH
5 STUDY
6 MASTER FOYER
7 HER MASTER BEDROOM
8 HER MASTER BATH
9 HER WARDROBE
10 HIS MASTER BEDROOM
11 HIS MASTER BATH
12 HIS WARDROBE
13 EXERCISE ROOM
14 MASSAGE ROOM
15 SAUNA
16 STEAM ROOM
17 EXERCISE BATH
18 EQUIPMENT ROOM
19 GRAND ROOM
20 DINING ROOM
21 WINE ROOM
22 KITCHEN
23 COOLER
24 UTILITY
25 GUEST SUITE
26 GUEST BATH
27 GARAGE
28 GOLF CARTS
29 GENERATOR ROOM
30 BRIDGE
31 COLONNADE
32 PORTICO CUPOLA
33 VERANDA
34 OUTDOOR KITCHEN
35 POOL BATH
36 POOL
37 SPA
38 KOI POND
39 STAFF QUARTERS
40 STAFF BATH
41 LIBRARY
42 LIBRARY DECK
43 DECK
44 MOTOR COURT
45 WATER FEATURE

rear view | Double doors lead from the separate master suites to an outdoor spa with views of the fairway. Stacked fieldstone creates a natural soaking pool, waterfall and stream that link to the main pool. At the roofline, a carved-stone rim encircles a cupola lined with a row of transoms that bring natural light indoors.

site plan | This plan features an unrestrained footprint that wraps a central courtyard and koi pond, announced by a grand portico. Casita-style guest suites straddle the forward gate, and a stone walkway leads to the formal entry. A splendid master wing includes an exercise and steam room, sauna, separate suites and a private study. At the opposite side of the plan, two secondary suites offer privacy and comfort. Outdoor spaces wrap the rear perimeter with a pool and a series of natural-rock spas.

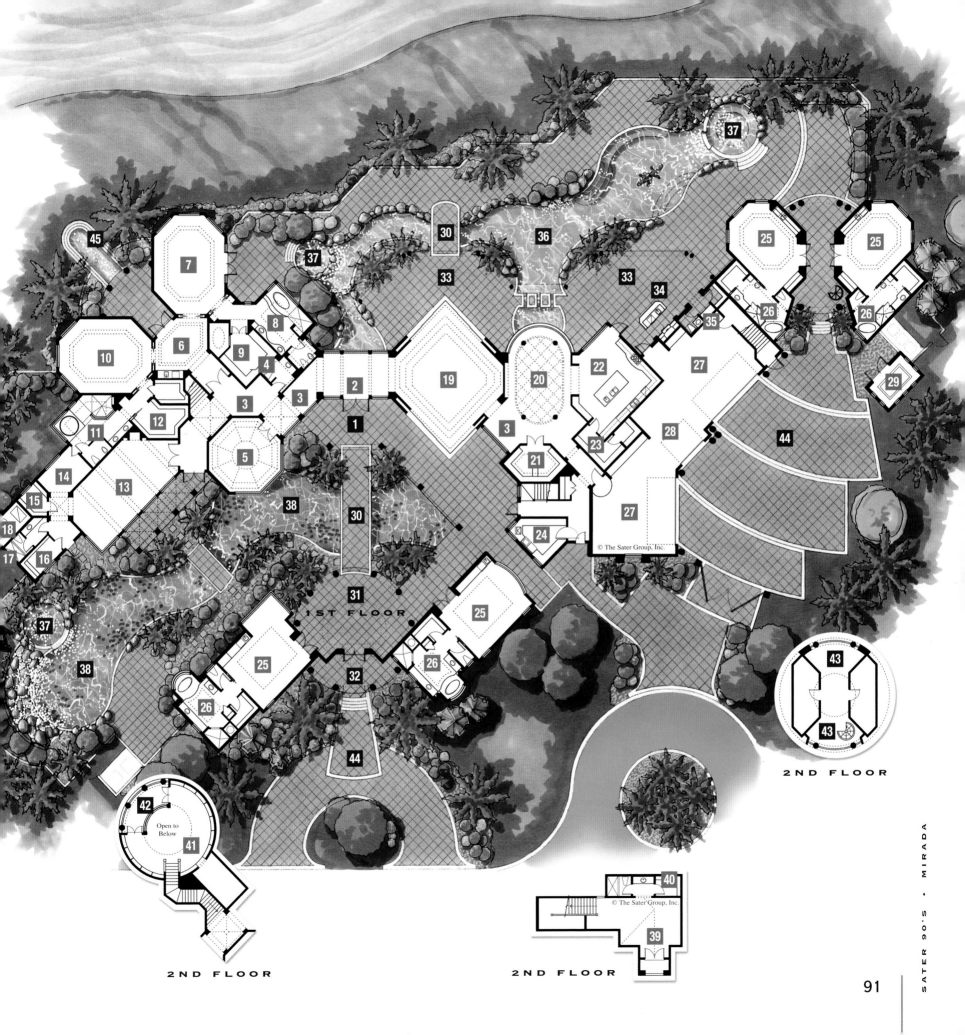

1ST FLOOR

2ND FLOOR

2ND FLOOR

2ND FLOOR

Open to Below

© The Sater Group, Inc.

© The Sater Group, Inc.

SATER TODAY
ELEGANCE DEFINED

Architecture today looks beautifully familiar.

Today, The Sater Group continues to employ proven design concepts, while developing better, inventive ways to define the American home. The challenge to create more than mere shelter requires an ability to craft spaces that intuitively respond and cater to the needs of its owners. The pursuit of creating a living environment has led to many design innovations, among them the "interactive space." These "spaces" or zones are clusters of rooms that function as a whole, unifying the home and bringing the owner and their guests together for important events or simply daily living.

Other innovations, such as cornerless sliding-glass walls, family valets or expanded utility, club rooms, walk-in showers and airy solanas, enhance the circulation or improve the function of a home, without losing an ounce of charm and beauty. Grand bays and robust pilasters, carved capitals and classic columns are at home here too.

Dan continually looks to lessons garnered from a rich past, with a diverse American vernacular derived from great classical architects such as Palladio, Latrobe, Hunt, and even Jefferson. Melding the distinctive marks of our heritage with houses that meet the needs of an evolved and rapidly diverse culture is a process carefully undertaken on every new home designed by The Sater Group. Dan seeks not to replicate but to incorporate these lessons in new proportions, detail and scale while implementing digital-age technologies and the latest amenities and materials.

The Sater Group continues to integrate lessons learned from its custom designs into a growing pre-designed homes portfolio, adapting plans for use in all regions and in all styles, seeking to fulfill Dan's desire to make good design available to all.

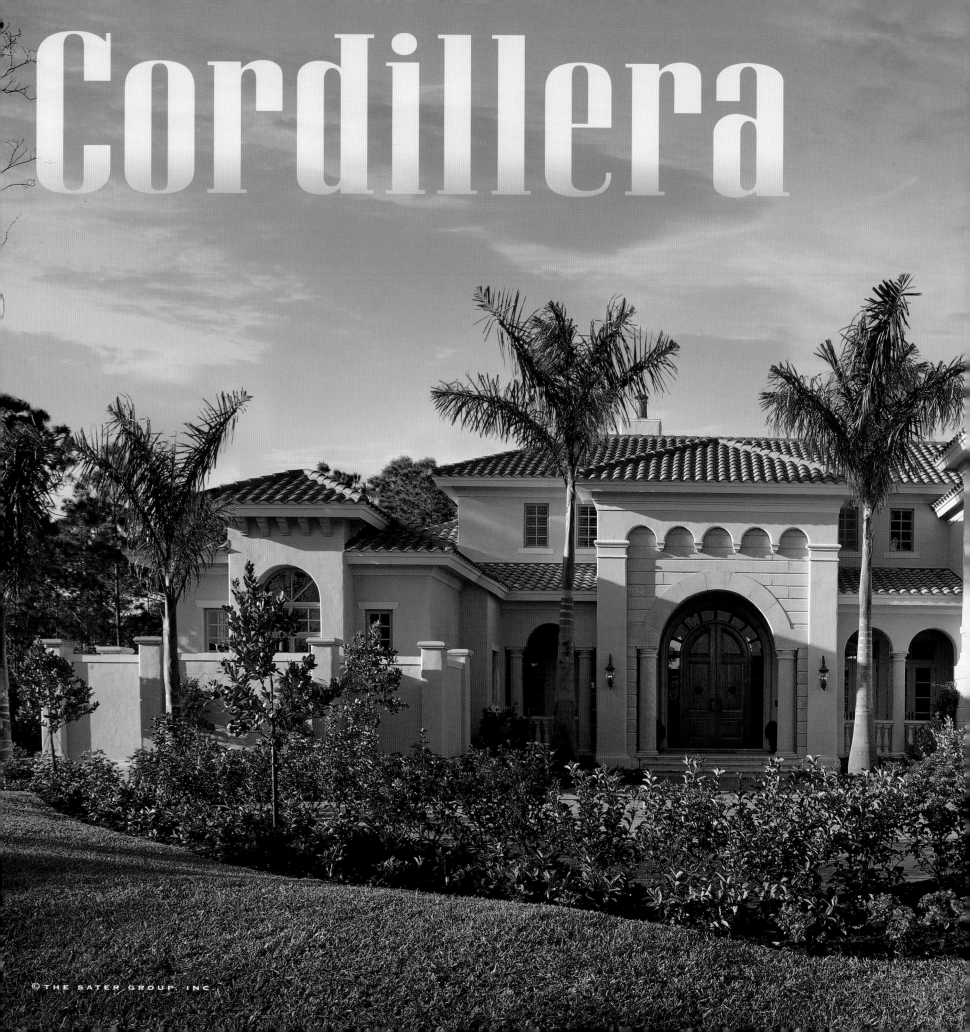

Cordillera

© THE SATER GROUP, INC

Scenery abounds in this elegant lakefront Spanish-style home.

dan's notes | *The desire to create a dwelling that paid homage to Palm Beach's great Spanish-influenced villas while embracing contemporary design ideas and technologies resulted in this grand Naples home. Incorporating modern amenities and elements such as cornerless disappearing sliding-glass walls, club rooms, outdoor living spaces and full-house automation make this home a place of relaxation and comfort unlike any other. I wanted to blend an authentic style with a sweeping Mediterranean theme, while staying true to my personal vision of home design.*

Several ports south of Sanibel Island, this Naples retreat offers a magnificent street presence, with a processional experience from the entry portico through a vaulted foyer to the grand central living space and wide views of the water. The façade's deeply recessed entry reflects an early 18th-century influence—a revival technique that draws on the elaborate treatment of doors and windows used in renaissance styles—set into dramatic high relief by a series of carved arches. Colossal pilasters, framed by a rusticated stone surround, lead through paneled doors to an outside-in arrangement of rooms, where sunlight mingles freely with the furnishings and the extremes of a subtropical climate are kept at bay by advanced climate controls.

A careful mixture of new and ancient elements creates the air of a Spanish *castilla* fortified with massive stone walls. With plenty of high-tech amenities, the house takes on a sense of the future, layered with the elaborate ornamentation of ages past.

LOCATION: NAPLES, FLORIDA

BUILDER: KURTZ HOMES

LANDSCAPE ARCHITECT:
OUTSIDE PRODUCTIONS, INC.
SCOTT WINDHAM, ASLA

INTERIOR DESIGN:
ACCESSORIES ETC., INC.

PHOTOGRAPHY BY: CJ WALKER

SATER TODAY • CORDILLERA

foyer/wet bar | The foyer poses richly articulated Corinthian columns and simple Tuscan pilasters in an unpretentious scheme that offers easy comfort and just enough drama. Wide open to the living room, the front gallery absorbs lakefront views that pour in through the rear wall of glass, illuminating the space and inspiring a sense of serenity. A long colonnade leads the eye toward a terminal vestibule— anchored by a paneled wet bar— which links the casual living area and service hall.

pool | Palm trees and beds of poppy-red geraniums in cut-stone planters border the freshwater lap pool, designed to extend the eye out to the lake beyond. An extensive sun terrace connects the outdoor living areas with a solana, spa and outdoor kitchen.

pool deck | Shapely columns and arches create a fluid boundary between the pool deck and solana, and shelter the outside living area from the midday sun. A large central gable enhanced with corbels and tall pilasters anchors the space and underscores the richly textured architectural themes of the home.

solana | A world apart from the bustle of the bay front, the outdoor retreat wraps the leisure room, nook and kitchen with a perfect space for entertaining. Interior and exterior living areas mix seamlessly via retreating glass doors, permitting an easy, ongoing dialogue with the landscape. Unaffected and fundamental, the solana includes an alfresco kitchen and massive stone fireplace. Sculpted wrought-iron bar chairs complement a rich cherrywood ceiling and environ-friendly recessed lighting.

leisure room | The plan's dedication to the natural environment dissolves the boundaries of inside and outside spaces, extending the long vistas of the leisure room to the sun terrace, solana and beyond. A soft neutral palette visually integrates the spaces with exotic mixes of textures and contrasting shades, selected for their aesthetic harmony with the grand scale of the area. High-end electronics integrated into the design provide surround-sound, advanced security systems and soft, subtle lighting.

living room | Double-paneled entry doors mirror the symmetry of the massive, intricately carved fireplace and stone surround at the formal center of the home. Straight ahead of the main entry, a series of three French doors open to a spectacular pool setting, offering brilliant views both day and night. An upper-level bridge overlooks, while connecting two guest suites, a game room, pub and home theater located above the garage.

master bath | Framed by twin Tuscan columns, a sculpted Persian-red marble tub surround subdues the grand scale of the owners' bath. Glimpses of the private garden mingle with daylight—or moonlight—allowed by a tall muntin window and fanlight. European cabinetry sets off vintage lamps that illuminate the vanity and her lavatory. Myriad textures, created by scumble-glazed walls, carved architectural forms and natural composites of marble, masonry and wood, enhance the retreat.

master bedroom | Floor-to-ceiling windows permit natural light to brighten the owners' bedroom during daytime hours and the stars at night. An extended wing provides a secluded sitting space that is perfect for light reading, conversation or a bit of privacy. Architectural treatments, such as curved moldings, a coffered ceiling and a flattened arch, lend dimension, depth and texture to the room, which leads outside to the sun terrace, spa and pool. A hand-sculpted niche is carved into the wall above the bed, iterating the curves of the arch-top windows and anchoring the neutral décor.

2nd floor bridge/hallway | Stunning maple-wood floors unify the varied levels and disparate schemes of the bridge connecting the upper-level guest suites. Dual wrought-iron railings overlook the foyer and living spaces below, and oppose the soothing leaf-green and buttercup hues of the hall and suites.

dining room | Tailored, classic furnishings lend a formal air to the space, which leads outdoors to the sun terrace. Connected to the living room at the center of the plan, the dining room takes in views of the pool and lakefront.

rear | Exquisite details enrich the central gable that dominates the rear perimeter of the home: an arcature caps the rusticated surround and massive pilasters frame the archway in complementary styles. A row of French doors opens the interior to the outside living area, which overlooks the sun terrace and pool. To the left, the solana dissolves the boundaries of outer and inner spaces and features a fireplace and alfresco kitchen.

study | For secluded spaces such as the study, versatility is vital. Closely linked to the living area via a shared fireplace, the room offers a quiet environment for talks and planning. Adjacent to the master wing, the study easily converts to a work space, reading room or home office. Double doors open to the sun terrace and pool, offering an easy transition from work to play.

solana | A unique mix of cherrywood, masonry and stone, the solana offers the outdoor living area more than just views. Infused with scenery, the structure both harbors guests for *plein air* parties and shelters them from bright sunlight.

Cordillera | SATER TODAY

© THE SATER GROUP, INC.

FRONT PERSEPECTIVE

site plan | Based on a neo-Mediterranean scheme with a modified Spanish context, the villa-style plan opens traditionally boxed spaces to easy breezes and satisfying views of the landscape. The vaulted foyer opens through the front gallery to the formal core of the home: a series of three view-oriented rooms designed to encourage quiet activities and friendly conversations. To the right of the home, the casual living zone incorporates a spacious leisure room that links with a morning bay and kitchen. Retreating glass walls maximize the glamorous character of the space, allowing an airy environment that's both impressive and highly comfortable. Upstairs, a balcony bridge overlooking the living area connects a game room, pub and home theater with two guest suites. Adjoining the solana to the rear of the plan, a cabana suite hosts live-in relatives or serves as a retreat for family members.

REAR ELEVATION

site plan legend

1 ENTRY PORTICO
2 FOYER
3 LIVING ROOM
4 STUDY
5 DINING ROOM
6 MASTER FOYER
7 MASTER BATH
8 HER WARDROBE
9 HIS WARDROBE
10 MASTER SUITE
11 MASTER SITTING
12 MASTER GARDEN
13 WET BAR
14 WINE CELLAR
15 POWDER BATH
16 NOOK
17 PANTRY
18 KITCHEN
19 LEISURE ROOM
20 COURTYARD
21 CABANA SUITE
22 CABANA POOL BATH
23 OUTDOOR KITCHEN
24 SOLANA
25 POOL
26 FOUNTAIN
27 SPA
28 SUN TERRACE
29 UTILITY ROOM
30 BRIDGE
31 GAME ROOM/PUB
32 GAME ROOM BATH
33 THEATER
34 BALCONY
35 GUEST BEDROOM #1
36 GUEST DECK #1
37 GUEST BATH #1
38 GUEST BEDROOM #2
39 GUEST DECK #2
40 GUEST BATH #2
41 STORAGE
42 2-CAR GARAGE
43 PORTE-COCHERE
44 MOTOR COURT

2ND FLOOR

1ST FLOOR

© The Sater Group, Inc.

Seabrook

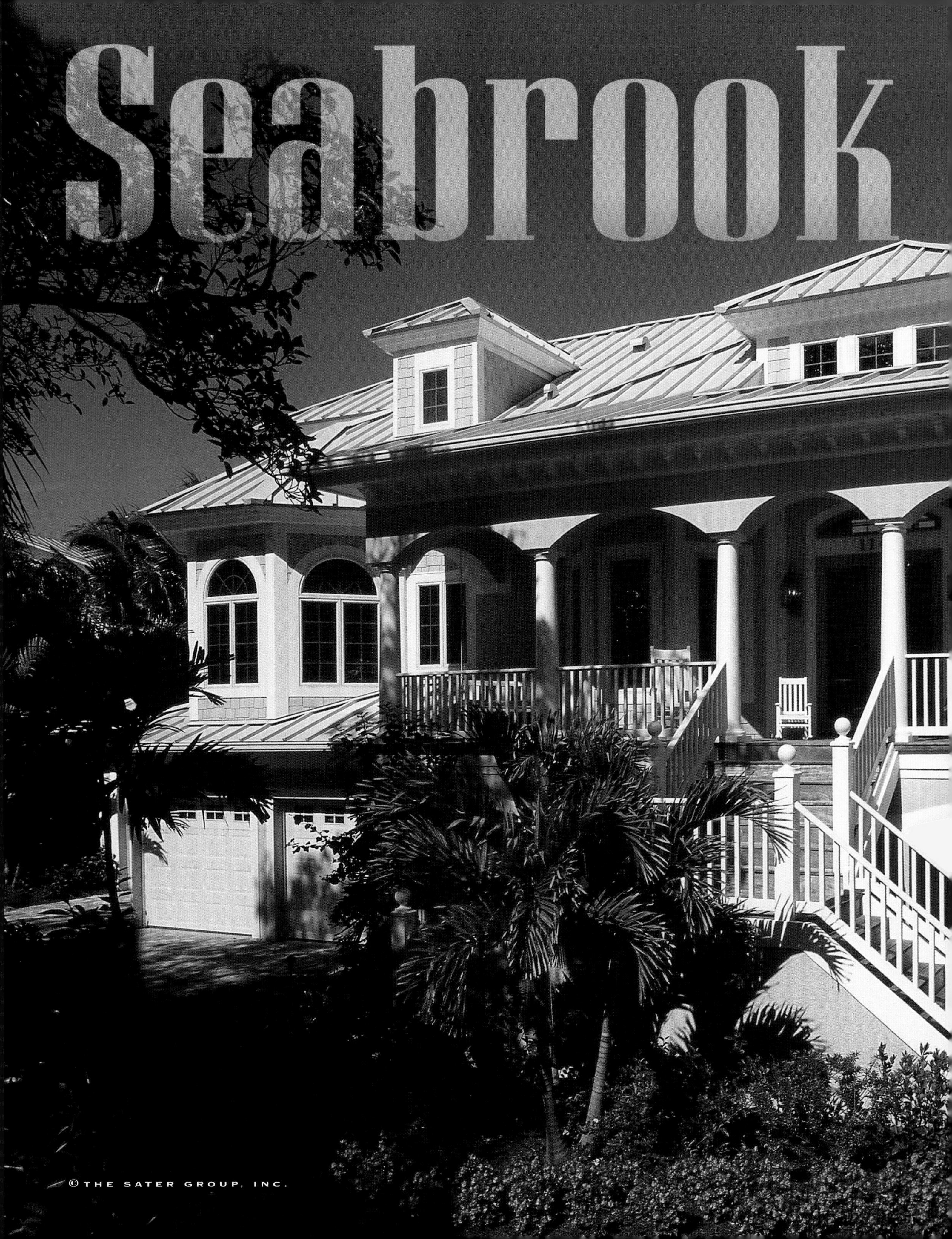

© THE SATER GROUP, INC.

Tradition-inspired island cottage makes a statement of its own.

dan's notes | *For me, this Sanibel Island location called for a lighthearted interpretation of the coastal vernacular infused with a relaxed, by-the-sea sensibility. High-spirited lines enliven the classical elements, with plenty of glass to let in daylight. Our clients envisioned an elegant yet casual home with great views of the water. They wanted function and flexibility and, above all, for a sense of intimacy to embrace the family members who dwelt within. This modern home is cozy and comfortable yet still exhilarating and inspiring.*

Layered with rough bisque shingles, pebble-hued stucco and a standing-seam roof, this waterfront home obeys the limits of coastal height restrictions yet is grandly scaled, with spacious rooms that boast enviable views throughout the interior. Infused with refined, well-crafted touches, the house achieves an upscale rhythm, with such dramatic features as exposed beam trusses and rich cherrywood floors. A splendid capacity for authentic detail is exhibited with evocative mixes of primal and classical elements.

Formality appears merely as a solitary element in the closely-knit fabric of inside and outside spaces. The grand symmetry conveyed by a series of arches at the front entry, many sets of French doors and rows of stately radius windows confer a near-reverent air upon the plan, without intruding on the prevailing informality of its rooms. Wide views, a palette of earthy textures, plush furnishings and calm, buttery hues define the sand-between-the-toes disposition of the interior.

LOCATION:
SANIBEL ISLAND, FLORIDA

BUILDER: BENCHMARK BUILDERS

LANDSCAPE ARCHITECT:
R.S. WALSH LANDSCAPING, INC.

INTERIOR DESIGN: ROBB & STUCKY
DEBORAH MAURER, ASID

PHOTOGRAPHY BY: CJ WALKER

great room | A trio of tall windows takes in views of Estero Bay and underscores the informality of exposed trusses, painted to match the neutral hues of the walls and wood trim. Rustic wood pieces subdue a bold blend of eclectic furnishings, set off by a wrought-iron chandelier. Hand-painted mosaic tiles contradict a gilded frame and deeply carved mantel above the fireplace.

office | Secluded to the front of the plan behind pocket doors, the office enjoys bay-window views of the entry porch and forward property. A beamed ceiling echoes the office shape and adds dimensionality.

master bedroom | Muntin windows in the bumped-out bay bring in plenty of natural light and views that extend across the water. A vaulted tongue-and-groove ceiling adds depth to the airy dimensions of the room, while two lateral windows allow glimpses of the lush side property.

kitchen | Wrapped with cream-white European cabinetry, the food-preparation area of the kitchen boasts high-end accoutrements, such as a six-burner cooktop. Vintage hanging lamps hover above an island counter, which features a rustic woodblock countertop, a dual vegetable sink and a service area for snacks and easy meals.

breakfast nook | Closest of all of the rooms to the water, the nook brings the architecture down to intimate scale with a modified tray ceiling, slender transoms and a bay of windows. Authentic wicker furnishings, a sisal rug and a plank floor help to capture the early spirit of the region.

guest bath | A guest suite features a flexible bath with a fanciful nautical theme. Placed near the private study and linked to a secondary bedroom via a pocket door, this convenient space offers linen storage and a view of the side property through louvered shutters. Dual pedestal sinks and porcelain fixtures complement a shelf for bath toys. Beadboard walls wrap the room, adding a touch of warmth and whimsy.

stairs | An art niche framing the foyer harbors an antique console and mirror, which reflects the angular lines of the stairway leading to the upper-level guest suites. Enhanced by period furnishings, travel mementos and treasures of the sea, the entry manages a relaxed disposition that's repeated throughout the home.

great room | Tuscan-order columns lend a neoclassical air to the vaulted center of the home. Simple forms—rows of transoms, a milk-white mantelpiece and hand-painted mosaic surround—complement a variety of pure elements: a plank dining table, hardwood floors and exposed trusses painted to match the room.

veranda | Softscapes surrounding the pool and spa border lush tropical growth that helps to seclude the property. A centered gable harbors a simple truss, which iterates the theme of the house: purity and open space. Turrets framing the veranda sport plenty of windows and lead to outdoor living areas with comfortable amenities of their own. Along the waterfront, tall bays and high-pitched roofs reflect the region's vernacular.

guest suite 1st floor | Exuberant blends of colors, shapes and textures compete only with glimpses of scenery in the main-level guest suite. Designed for guests who plan to stay awhile, the room features ample wardrobe space and leads out to a quiet area of the front porch — a perfect spot for morning juice or tea. A pocket door leads to a bath with linen storage, while a private vestibule connects the space to a secluded study with access to the pool and spa.

guest suite #4 | A savory palette of floral patterns and pastels deck out a remote, upper-level guest suite, which boasts a walk-in closet, private hall with window seat and a computer niche just right for books or a laptop. Louvered shutters both protect the space from the midday sun and permit natural light to illuminate the vibrant décor. A kitsch lamp adds a circle of incandescent light to the nightstand.

front entry | Framed with lush vegetation and tropical
growth, the approach to the formal entry is lined with a series
of simple balustrades that set off the streetscape and evoke
visions of Americana's white picket fences. Sheltered by a deep
overhang, the paneled glass doors leading to the foyer repeat
a variety of rectilinear forms that enliven the streetscape.

veranda stairs | A winding wooden stairway leads down to
an idyllic pool and spa arena enriched by a surround of textured
pavers. Simple balustrades line the open veranda and descend to
a pedestrian path which leads to the sea. Beyond the beach, a
primitive pier serves as a port for passing boats and a launch
point for adventurous swimmers.

Seabrook | SATER TODAY

site plan | A sleek update on the neighborhood's traditional seaside vernacular, the multilevel plan steps toward the sea following the flow of the land, with extensive sculpted edges carefully set into the lush topography. Upper-level decks frame a wide-open veranda that absorbs scenery and affords light in the adjoining living spaces: the kitchen, nook, great room and study. With a vaulted center, the plan creates an airy arena, flexible enough for outdoor activities. Rooms with floor-to-ceiling windows offer treehouse views of the water and complement the cozier, more intimate spaces of the home.

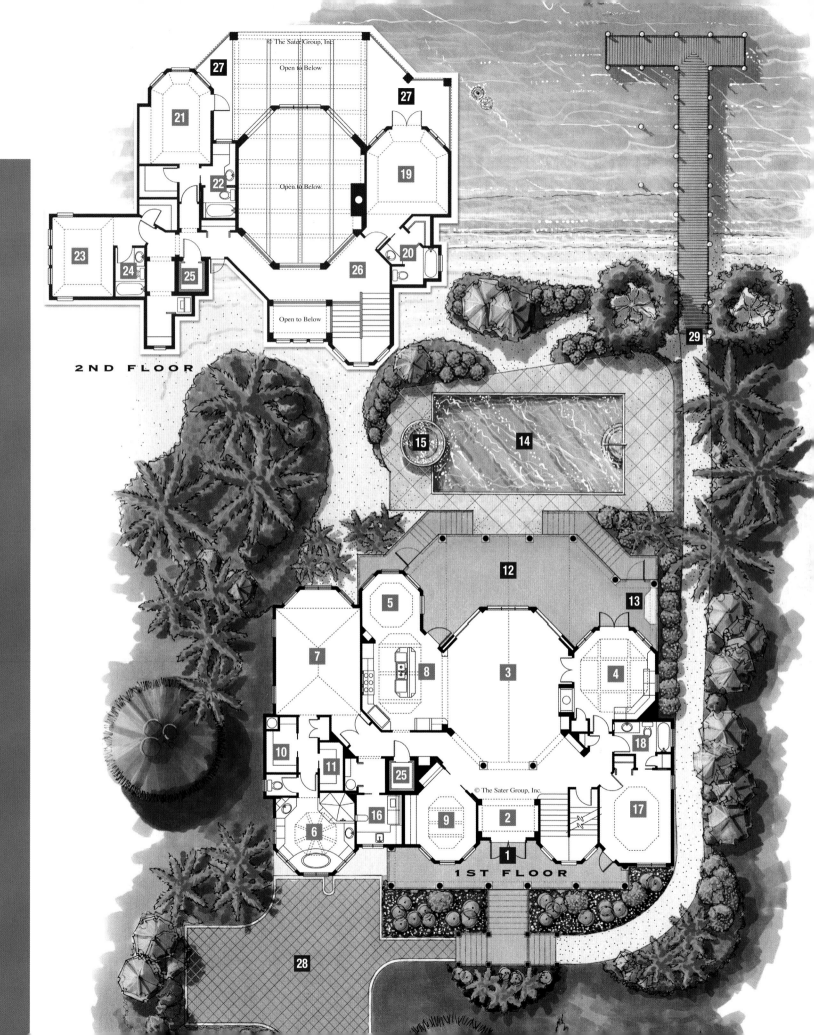

site plan legend

1 ENTRY
2 FOYER
3 GREAT ROOM
4 STUDY
5 NOOK
6 MASTER BATH
7 MASTER SUITE
8 KITCHEN
9 OFFICE
10 HER WARDROBE
11 HIS WARDROBE
12 VERANDA
13 OUTDOOR KITCHEN
14 POOL
15 SPA
16 UTILITY ROOM
17 GUEST SUITE #1
18 GUEST BATH #1
19 GUEST SUITE #2
20 GUEST BATH #2
21 GUEST SUITE #3
22 GUEST BATH #3
23 GUEST SUITE #4
24 GUEST BATH #4
25 ELEVATOR
26 LOFT
27 DECK
28 MOTOR COURT
29 DOCK

LOWER LEVEL:
2-CAR GARAGE

2ND FLOOR

1ST FLOOR

© The Sater Group, Inc.

Open to Below

Salina

© THE SATER GROUP, INC.

Old World charm enriches a modern palatial villa.

dan's notes | *In this home—perhaps more than in many others—the living areas relate to one another in a particularly meaningful way. The dining room and parlor, for example, connect via a gallery that brings light to both spaces and creates an atmosphere that invites people to mingle. Enabling the client to entertain great groups of family and guests comfortably was a primary focus for me, as well as connecting indoor zones with outer living areas and great views.*

Nested amid panoramas so wide they easily reveal the gentle curve of the earth, this European-style villa fits its pristine location seamlessly. The refined elevation faces a frontier of preserved wetlands and straddles the lush, subtropical fairways of a local golf club. A deeply recessed entry leads to an open arrangement of the foyer, parlor and formal dining room—a vaulted arena defined by massive stone columns—and takes in wide views of the pool and rear property. The stair hall creates an easy transition from the traditional spaces to a well-organized yet wide-open casual retreat, which includes a capacious leisure room designed for large informal gatherings. A media room opens to the outdoors and links closely to a portico and solana, warmed by a fireplace.

At the opposite end of the house, the owners' retreat features a coffered ceiling, private sitting area and sumptuous master bath. On the second level, owners have the benefit of a secluded study, another sitting area and an observation deck, while guests enjoy their own scenery-infused loft and sun deck. A spectacular tower loft caps the third story of the stair tower and offers panoramic views of the countryside.

LOCATION: NAPLES, FLORIDA

BUILDER: KURTZ HOMES

LANDSCAPE ARCHITECT:
OUTSIDE PRODUCTIONS, INC.

INTERIOR DESIGN:
ACCESSORIES ETC., INC.

PHOTOGRAPHY BY: CJ WALKER

parlor |

In a room designed for quiet conversation, ornate Corinthian columns sentinel a refined mix of hues and textures inspired by Greek and Roman antiquities. A coffered ceiling lends depth to this formal space, which leads via French doors to a lanai and decorative steps across the pool. Linked by a gallery, the parlor and dining room share the warmth offered by the fireplace.

wine cellar/stairs |

Just off the foyer, and connected to the dining room via a butler's pantry, an extensive wine rack built under the stairs companions an intricate paneled door leading back to the storage cellar. A graceful, wrought-iron balustrade enlivens carved-stone stairs that link the main level with the tower loft.

dining room | With a splendid view of the gardens, pool and spa, the formal dining room benefits from placement to the rear of the home. Graceful arches and stately columns provide an open boundary with the entry foyer and galleries, and intricately carved capitals connect past and present.

stair view | Climbing three stories from the foyer to the lookout tower, stone stairs wind through a forward turret, linking public space with a quiet area intended just for one or two.

pool deck | Carefully positioned near the leisure room and nook, two sets of garden tables and tea chairs invite alfresco dining by the pool. Stone steps cross the water to link the casual outdoor sitting and dining space with the owners' loggia. Nearby, a set of French doors opens the parlor to fresh air and poolside breezes.

rear pool view | Versatile seating areas line the pool and rear perimeter, adapted to the owners' tastes for an intimate, comfortable scale—even for crowd-size gatherings. Serenity prevails in this outdoor setting, defined by traditional columns and a simple balustrade lining the sun deck above the leisure room. The home's openness and flexibility allow guests and family to mingle informally indoors and out.

master bedroom | Sophisticated lighting enhances mood and color in the owners' private retreat. A bayed alcove harbors a sitting area that boasts panoramic views and leads to the loggia. Sculpted arches and a stepped tray ceiling lend elements of texture and depth, and the deeply carved walnut furnishings balance the neutral palette. Two sets of glass doors open the room to the outside and permit breezes during daylight and twilight hours.

master sitting | The owners' love of period chandeliers and table lamps adds a classic flair to their own sitting space. Buttercream walls warm the intimate bay without competing with the sun's rays seeping through the louvered shutters.

master bath | Luxury abounds in a stunning angled bath centered on a dramatic sienna-marble tub. Surrounded by a series of structural columns, the bay overlooks a garden defined by a wood trellis, offering an air of tranquility to the high-glam ambience of the bath. A fine mix of beauty and function, the room encompasses separate areas for two owners and allows scenery and sunlight— or moonlight—to illuminate its spaces.

master morning bar | Tea and coffee are served in the master suite, with a morning kitchen that eases the owners' daily routine. Glass-faced cabinets and a beadboard backsplash enhanced by earth-toned granite countertops and paneled cabinetry create the at-home feeling the owners desired for this private setting.

Salina | SATER TODAY

130

site plan | Designed in a grand Mediterranean style, this expansive villa employs walls of glass and rows of windows to take in beautiful views of the surrounding estuary. Five-star fairways wind through the region, enhancing the plan's picturesque backdrop. A grand foyer divides the common areas from the master retreat, offering the owners solitude and sanctuary. The rear perimeter of the home melds a widely diverse blend of outdoor functions, with shoes-off poolside sitting areas, an alfresco kitchen, a fireside solana linked to a portico, and serene lanais with private views. A side staircase leads to the owners' study, sitting space and sun deck, while the foyer stairs climb two levels to a tower loft offering panoramic vistas of the area.

site plan legend

1 PORTICO
2 FOYER
3 PARLOR
4 STUDY
5 DINING ROOM
6 MASTER BATH
7 MASTER SUITE
8 MASTER SITTING
9 HER WARDROBE
10 HIS WARDROBE
11 WET BAR
12 POWDER BATH
13 NOOK
14 BUTLER'S PANTRY
15 KITCHEN
16 LEISURE ROOM
17 GUEST SUITE
18 GUEST BATH
19 POOL BATH
20 OUTDOOR KITCHEN
21 SOLANA
22 POOL
23 FOUNTAIN
24 SUN DECK
25 UTILITY ROOM
26 MEDIA ROOM
27 DECK
28 SITTING
29 BEDROOM #1
30 BATH #1
31 BEDROOM #2
32 BATH #2
33 LOFT
34 GALLERY
35 LOGGIA
36 3-CAR GARAGE
37 PORT-COCHERE
38 OUTDOOR FIREPLACE
39 MORNING BAR
40 SPA
41 MOTOR COURT
42 TOWER
43 WINE CELLAR
44 WATER FEATURE

1ST FLOOR

2ND FLOOR

Open to Below

© The Sater Group, Inc.

Rafina

© THE SATER GROUP, INC

Time-honored lines step into a 21st-century vision.

dan's notes | *This design takes advantage of its prime inland location with an orientation of the rear perimeter toward a lake and scenic fairway. In order to truly make use of the site, I designed the home to incorporate rooms surrounded by glass that grants an 180-degree view of the water, golf course and preserve. The strategy works throughout the plan by connecting the rooms with sight lines that extend beyond the client's property. Every unique space in the home— including the guest suites—has a view and an easy link to the outdoors.*

At first glance, the deeply recessed and highly decorated entry of this very modern plan may seem the stylish introduction to an elegant Italian villa, yet it is a skillful reinvention of the past. The remarkable transformation of arched, rusticated forms into a graceful façade with a pedestrian-friendly approach expresses the owners' desire for an inviting retreat where friends are always welcome. Past the paneled entry doors, floors turn unexpectedly from lustrous tiles in the forward gallery to timber planks—recouped from antique buildings—in the formal rooms. Casual areas such as the leisure and game rooms are paired with outdoor living spaces for a shoes-off sensibility that is right at home in a design strategy that brings sun decks and plasma screens together with a refined sense of history.

Breathtaking views dominate the upper-level guest wing, which provides two light-filled suites, a loft and a wide deck overlooking the pool. The interior speaks to a carefree life of low-key elegance and fresh lakefront breezes.

LOCATION: NAPLES, FLORIDA

BUILDER: KURTZ HOMES

LANDSCAPE ARCHITECT:
OUTSIDE PRODUCTIONS, INC.
SCOTT WINDHAM, ASLA

INTERIOR DESIGN:
ACCESSORIES ETC., INC.

PHOTOGRAPHY BY: CJ WALKER

133

entry foyer | As modern as it is historic, the plan begins with an elegant paneled door that defies the past with sleek curved sidelights. An airy, barrel-vaulted foyer connects the public spaces and eases transitions to more secluded areas of the home. An eclectic theme plays checkered marble tiles against random stone pavers in the hall, and an elaborate gilt mirror counters a rustic period chest suited to a colonial scheme.

porte-cochere | An elaborate recessed entry lined with decorative brackets sets off a hipped tile roof and cupola, which provide the definitive elements of the plan's Italianate roots. The rusticated surround enriches authentic details such as carved corbels and corner quoins, and repeats the arched forms of the colonnades. At the front of the courtyard, an ornate vessel-shaped fountain announces the processional experience to the entry.

135

grand salon | A masterpiece of simplicity, the glass-walled grand salon exhibits open, unrestrained space anchored by a two-story fireplace and breathtaking views. Beyond a trio of radius windows and French doors, glimpses of the fountain, pool and spa bring in a sense of nature. A deeply carved cherry mantel captures the focus of the room.

study | An extension of the master suite, the study supports a library collection of favorite novels and art books. Wood-paneled walls lend an air of warmth and comfort in the owners' study, which serves as both a work place and an intimate setting for conversation.

kitchen | Exposed timber beams and a tongue-and-groove cypress ceiling animate the rustic qualities of the high-tech kitchen. The mosaic tile backsplash echoes the pattern of a decorative platter above the cooktop, collected from the owners' travels. Beyond the food-prep area is a butler's pantry, which leads to the dining room.

dining room | Entertaining around a carved anigre dining table is made elegantly simple with a nearby butler's pantry and the kitchen just beyond. Deep-red velvet drapes outline the artful views of an elegant covered deck framed by strong tapered columns.

master bedroom |
Amber-glazed walls create an envelope of calm in the owners' retreat, which includes a sitting bay with views of the pool and rear property. Floor-to-ceiling damask drapes soften the tall windows that surround the cozy master sitting area. To the right of the bay, French doors lead outside to a secluded part of the loggia shared only with the study.

master bath |
Every inch as grand as the rest of the house, the owners' bath features splendid amenities, such as a garden tub harbored by a bumped-out bay. Elegant columns sentinel a large bow window overlooking a carefully organized landscape. Sable-colored marble surrounds the spa-style tub, and candle-light mimics the glow of a vintage gilt chandelier.

Rafina | SATER TODAY

rear view | High arches wrap the screen-enclosed pool-and-spa arena, visually uniting the outer zone with the rear elevation. Trees, both planted and native, surround the space with welcome shade during midday hours. The loggia harbors flexible sitting areas, while the upper porch belongs to a game room designed for both family and guests.

site plan | With the rear perimeter sited toward a lake and serene, lush green fairways, the plan takes on an attitude of luxury, yet maintains an informal spirit from the grand entry to the infinity-edge pool. A curved trellis links the motor court and garages, and a path to the fountain—a symbol of welcome to visitors—leads to paneled front doors. Wide-open leisure spaces erase boundaries between indoors and out, while three splendid guest suites rival the beauty of the master retreat. The upper-level loft connects a techno-smart home theatre to a guest wing, which boasts its own game room and sun deck.

142

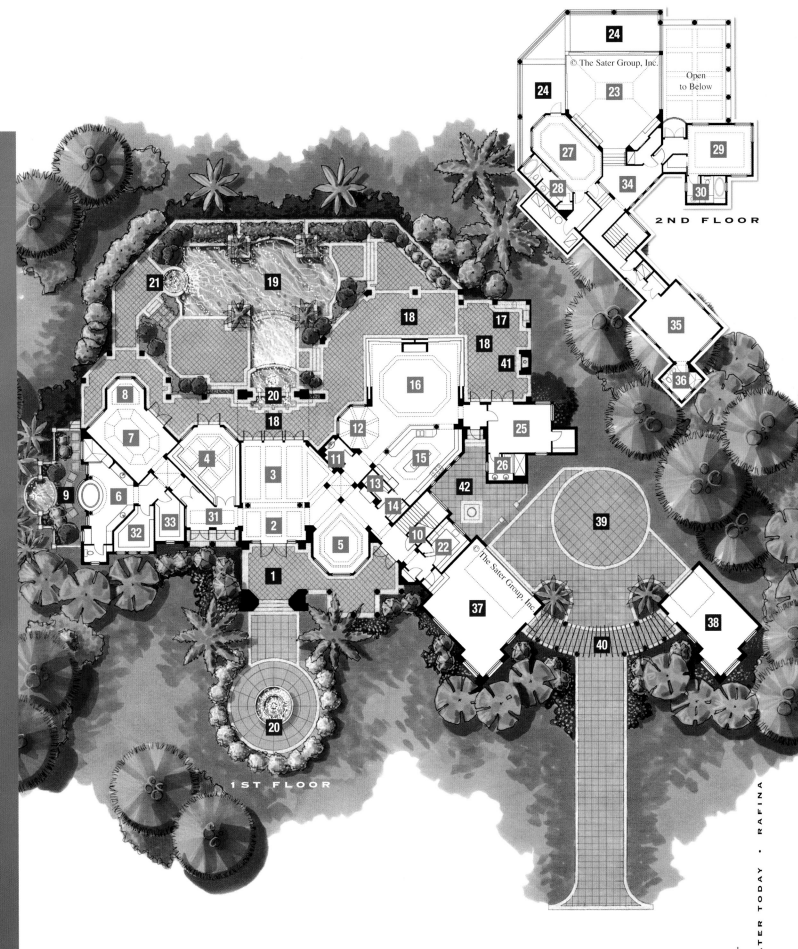

site plan legend

1 PORTICO
2 FOYER
3 GRAND SALON
4 STUDY
5 DINING ROOM
6 MASTER BATH
7 MASTER SUITE
8 MASTER SITTING
9 MASTER GARDEN
10 WINE CELLAR
11 POWDER BATH
12 NOOK
13 PANTRY
14 BUTLER'S PANTRY
15 KITCHEN
16 LEISURE ROOM
17 OUTDOOR KITCHEN
18 LOGGIA
19 POOL
20 FOUNTAIN
21 SPA
22 UTILITY ROOM
23 GAME ROOM
24 UPPER PORCH
25 GUEST SUITE #1
26 GUEST BATH #1
27 GUEST SUITE #2
28 GUEST BATH #2
29 GUEST SUITE #3
30 GUEST BATH #3
31 GALLERY
32 HER WARDROBE
33 HIS WARDROBE
34 LOFT
35 MEDIA ROOM
36 MEDIA BATH
37 2-CAR GARAGE
38 1-CAR GARAGE
39 MOTOR COURT
40 PERGOLA
41 FIREPLACE
42 SIDE ENTRY COURT

2ND FLOOR

© The Sater Group, Inc.

Open to Below

© The Sater Group, Inc.

1ST FLOOR

143

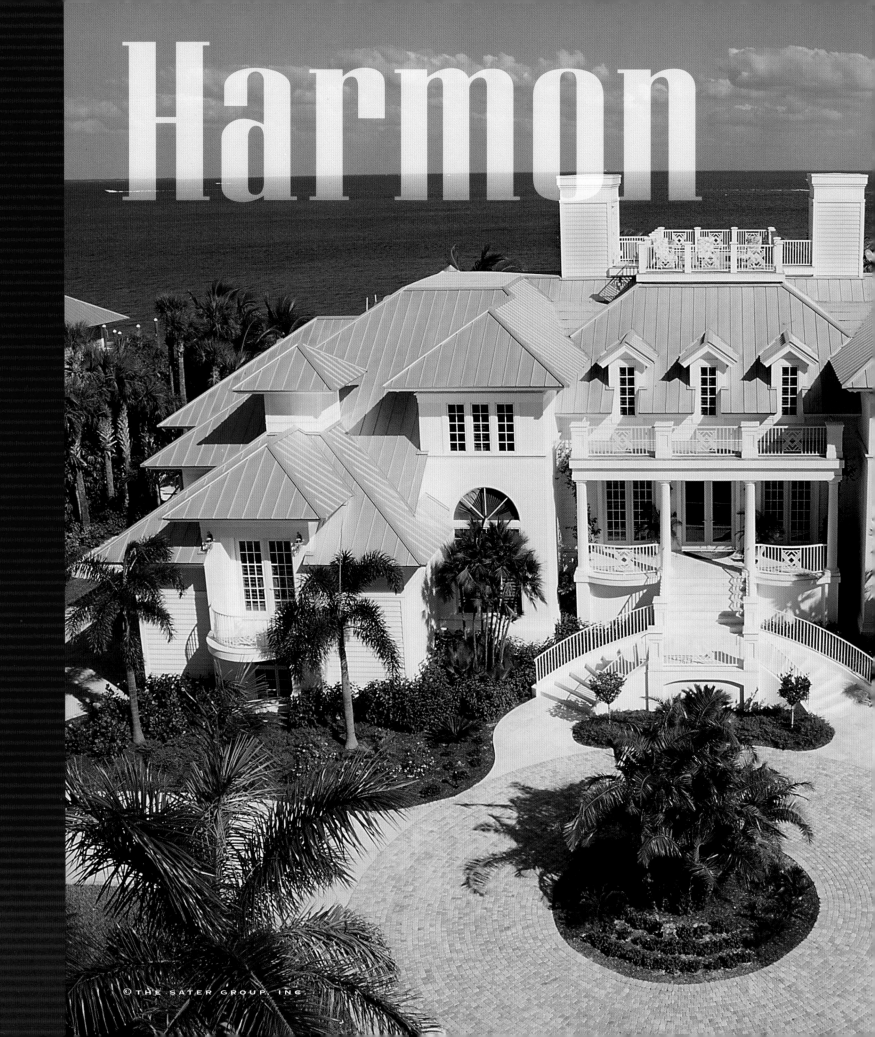

Harmon

© THE SATER GROUP, INC.

Classic Southern retreat reinvents Gulf Coast tradition.

dan's notes | *This is a grand coastal plan—drawn on regional tradition—with strong symmetry along the elevation. Classical columns and broad porticos give this home an elegant appearance—yet the home provides a casual experience. The rooftop deck offers spectacular overlooks of the Gulf and harbor, while a formal entry confirms the history of the architecture. At its core, I wanted the house to provide relaxed living for its owners, all the while soothing their appetites for scenic beauty by affording front-to-back views through French doors. With two spacious guest wings and an in-law suite, the plan functions well as a family retreat, where spontaneous gatherings are celebrated.*

Set toward the Gulf of Mexico and nested on the shores of Charlotte Harbor, the house enjoys a coveted island locale with views in every direction. Highly visible from the bayside, the design boasts an impressive rear elevation with a two-story gable and colonnade. Symetrical elements radiate from the front entry, while a standing-seam metal roof cascades in a variety of hips and gables. Wrapping porticos and a wide veranda integrate the house with its waterfront site, infusing the rooms with fresh air and a breezy, seafront disposition. Five guest suites offer a sense of welcome to the owners' family and friends, while the upper level provides a private retreat.

LOCATION:
BOCA GRANDE, FLORIDA

BUILDER:
SAFETY HARBOR HOMES, INC.

LANDSCAPE ARCHITECT:
OUTSIDE PRODUCTIONS, INC.
SCOTT WINDHAM, ASLA

INTERIOR DESIGN:
MYRNA GARBINS DESIGNS

PHOTOGRAPHY BY:
CJ WALKER

front porch | Facing the Gulf of Mexico across a wetlands preserve, the front elevation features a grand porch announced by a series of Doric columns and a pair of sweeping staircases. Lined with intricate metal balustrades, the porch railing pattern is repeated along the upper portico and roofline. Asymmetrical towers offer a subtle variation of the neoclassical theme, enhanced with vertical tongue-and-groove siding.

back porch | Oriented toward Charlotte Harbor, the veranda wraps the unrestrained rear perimeter of the house. Grand colonnades skirt the boundaries of the veranda, creating a sense of shelter without interfering with a breathtaking panorama of the water. Conceived as a house that would always be filled with family and friends, the plan incorporates two remote guest wings that frame the poolside retreat.

great room | Leaded-glass entry doors framed by mirroring windows allow natural light and glimpses of scenery to fill the hall and great room. Round tapered columns support graceful slump arches, while the scalloped edge above the bridge repeats the form of the colonnade below, creating a sense of unity.

kitchen | Beautifully designed to serve a variety of occasions as well as easy, everyday meals, the kitchen pairs European paneled cabinetry with sleek, stainless-steel appliances and maple-plank hardwood floors. With a food-preparation area large enough for two cooks, the island counter is positioned at the center of a space open to both the great room and nook.

kitchen/bar | A hand-painted backsplash in pale yellow and sea blue sets the palette for accent furnishings that line the snack counter, which also serves as a pass-through to the great room. The carved hood above the cooktop is a focal point for the kitchen, while the niche above the bar seating harbors a sunburst.

rear view | Greater than the sum of its parts, a magnificent hip extends the rear elevation to the edge of the spa and pool, enlisting a series of massive columns and a straightforward entablature to create a blissful retreat. Fanlights above the trio of windows create a soft complement to the dominant lines of the covered veranda.

great room | Views of Charlotte Harbor contribute a sense of serenity and calm to the great room, while French doors framing a trio of tall windows capture cool sea breezes. Deeply recessed tongue-and-groove panels contrast with a white-beamed coffered ceiling. A carved, two-story chimney creates a focus for the space, enhancing the mantel and stone surround.

Harmon | SATER TODAY

site plan | Steps from a private beach and pier, the layered pool deck wraps the edge of a wide veranda. Quiet sitting areas define the outdoor spaces of the perimeter, approaching the sea at the wings and retreating to screen-protected arcades near the interior. At the front of the plan, the entry hall, great room, nook and kitchen form the public area, which serves to separate the guest quarters. Upper-level square footage is dedicated to the master suite and study, each of which includes a sun deck. Stairs lead up from the bridge to a rooftop deck where views extend to the horizon.

site plan legend

1 PORTICO
2 HALL
3 GREAT ROOM
4 KITCHEN
5 BREAKFAST NOOK
6 DINING ROOM
7 MAIN GALLERY
8 PANTRY
9 ELEVATOR
10 POWDER BATH
11 UTILITY ROOM
12 STORAGE
13 GUEST SUITE #1
14 GUEST BATH #1
15 GUEST SUITE #2
16 GUEST BATH #2
17 GAME ROOM
18 GUEST SUITE #3
19 GUEST BATH #3
20 GUEST SUITE #4
21 GUEST BATH #4
22 GUEST SUITE #5
23 GUEST BATH #5
24 UPPER GALLERY
25 STUDY
26 DECK
27 MECHANICAL ROOM
28 BRIDGE
29 MASTER BEDROOM
30 MASTER SITTING
31 MASTER BATH
32 MASTER WARDROBE
33 OFFICE
34 VERANDA
35 OUTDOOR KITCHEN
36 SPA
37 POOL
38 SUN DECK
39 DOCK
40 MOTOR COURT

LOWER LEVEL:
TWO 3-CAR GARAGES

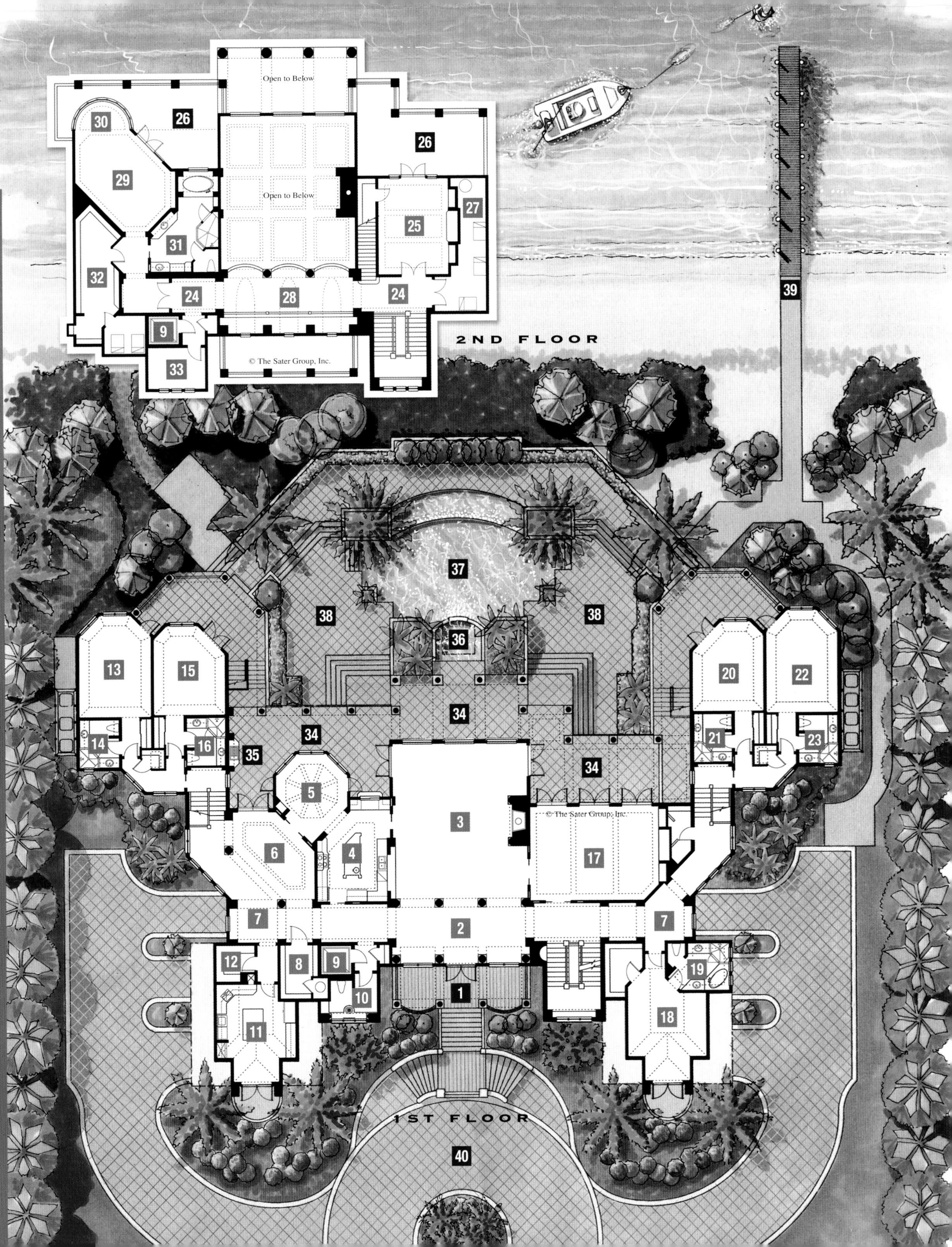

Open to Below
Open to Below
© The Sater Group, Inc.
2ND FLOOR
© The Sater Group, Inc.
1ST FLOOR

Belisima

© THE SATER GROUP, INC.

Elegant courtyard villa revisits early Mediterranean themes.

dan's notes | *Drawn on early Spanish styles, this plan features evocative details, such as broadly overhanging eaves and a concrete-tiled roof lined with deeply carved brackets. Oriented to take advantage of the Gulf of Mexico, this home is designed so that each room captures that view, while a side family entry increases the pattern of circulation through the guest wing. The rear elevation encompasses a distinctive tower, which provides an opportunity to beautify the interior with a rotunda and stairs. Working with a classic vocabulary, I wanted to throw an emphatic curve into the grand scheme, and create a place where the spaces relate to one another in practical ways.*

Sited among a lush landscape, this Mediterranean courtyard plan integrates an Italian Renaissance revival scheme with the more rugged elements of a country villa. Wide arched doorways, sleek marble surrounds, sweeping stairways and sculpted galleries embellish the interior and lend a sense of formality to the home, countering rough timber beams and terracotta floors. Impeccably classic details heighten the elegance of deeply comfortable rooms, which find easy transitions to the robust décor of the outdoor environment. The central rotunda connects the public realm with an upper-level game and guest wing, which opens to a wide deck overlooking the pool, veranda and koi pond.

LOCATION: NAPLES, FLORIDA

BUILDER: HUNT CONSTRUCTION

LANDSCAPE ARCHITECT:
FAIRVIEW LANDSCAPE

INTERIOR DESIGN:
VINCE MULLER & ASSOCIATES

PHOTOGRAPHY BY:
JOSEPH LAPEYRA

study | Lancet arches signal a Venetian influence in a room designed for contemplation. Views to the front property maintain a connection with the colonial architecture of the plan and bring in a sense of the outdoors.

porte-cochere/entry | A massive freestanding arcade sentinels the spacious courtyard leading to the entry. Robust masonry piers and columns contrast with an intricate wrought-iron gate, which relates in a revival scheme to a pleasing sculpted fountain.

stairs | Gravity-defying forms define a grand, sweeping staircase that connects the main-level gallery with the game room. A sculpted edge soars above a carved vestibule leading to the wine cellar.

living room | This grand-scale living room impresses immediately upon entry. A striking two-story fireplace framed in carved marble, competes with spectacular views beyond a set of glass doors.

kitchen | Antique cypress beams hover above the food-preparation area in the kitchen, which boasts granite countertops and new-century appliances. A tumbled-stone stove hood provides an earthy element to this ultra sophisticated kitchen.

butler's pantry | Designed to link easily with the formal dining room, wine cellar and kitchen, the butler's pantry includes a vegetable sink, counter space and plenty of storage. The décor matches the textures and tones of the kitchen, creating a sense of unity that runs through the nook and leisure room.

master foyer | Double pecky cypress doors lead into the master foyer. At the terminus of the private gallery, a sculpted art niche harbors an antique chest and gilt mirror. The groin-vault ceiling adds a touch of revival spirit and softens the edges of the master foyer.

game room | A grand rotunda links the main level with the game room, designed as a marvelous getaway for family members and guests. An intricate custom chandelier complements the wrought-iron balusters of the railing that frame and support the circular staircase. A complete wet bar provides refreshments for pool sharks and big-time gamers.

master bedroom | Fanlight windows, carved corbels and intricate ceiling coffers complement Hispanic influences even in the quiet spaces of the home, such as the owners' private retreat. Sculpted arches add depth and dimension to the room, and a peninsular fireplace borders a sitting area framed by views of the side and rear properties. Sliding glass doors open the master bedroom to the veranda and views of the coastal preserve.

veranda | Open to the leisure room and deck, the veranda features a sheltered outdoor eating area. Massive columns provide definition for the *plein air* retreat, and permit scenery and sunlight to infuse the space. Side chairs frame a cut-stone table with a *fleur-de-lys* pattern embellishing the pedestal. To the left, a fireplace with a carved mahogany-and-stone surround anchors a plush sitting area.

Belisima | SATER TODAY

pool deck | An arcade of flattened arches spans the rear deck, providing a subtle separation between the lush green fairway and the owners' pool and spa. Processional sight lines define a series of interlocking spaces: the outdoor sitting area links to the leisure room through retreating glass doors, extending the livability of the home; a wood-beamed pergola shelters the alfresco kitchen; and an open deck invites swimmers into the water. Stone steps lead to the top of the fountain, which harbors the spa.

164

site plan | True to its Moorish roots, the plan begins with a quatrefoil fountain and a gated courtyard, which increases the home's circulation via a side entry leading to guest quarters. The vaulted foyer serves as a fluid boundary between the front perimeter and the formal living room, which opens to a wrapping veranda. The rear tower encloses a rotunda and stairs linking the main level to a splendid club room with a sun deck. Retreating doors permit a transition from the leisure room to comfortable outside spaces.

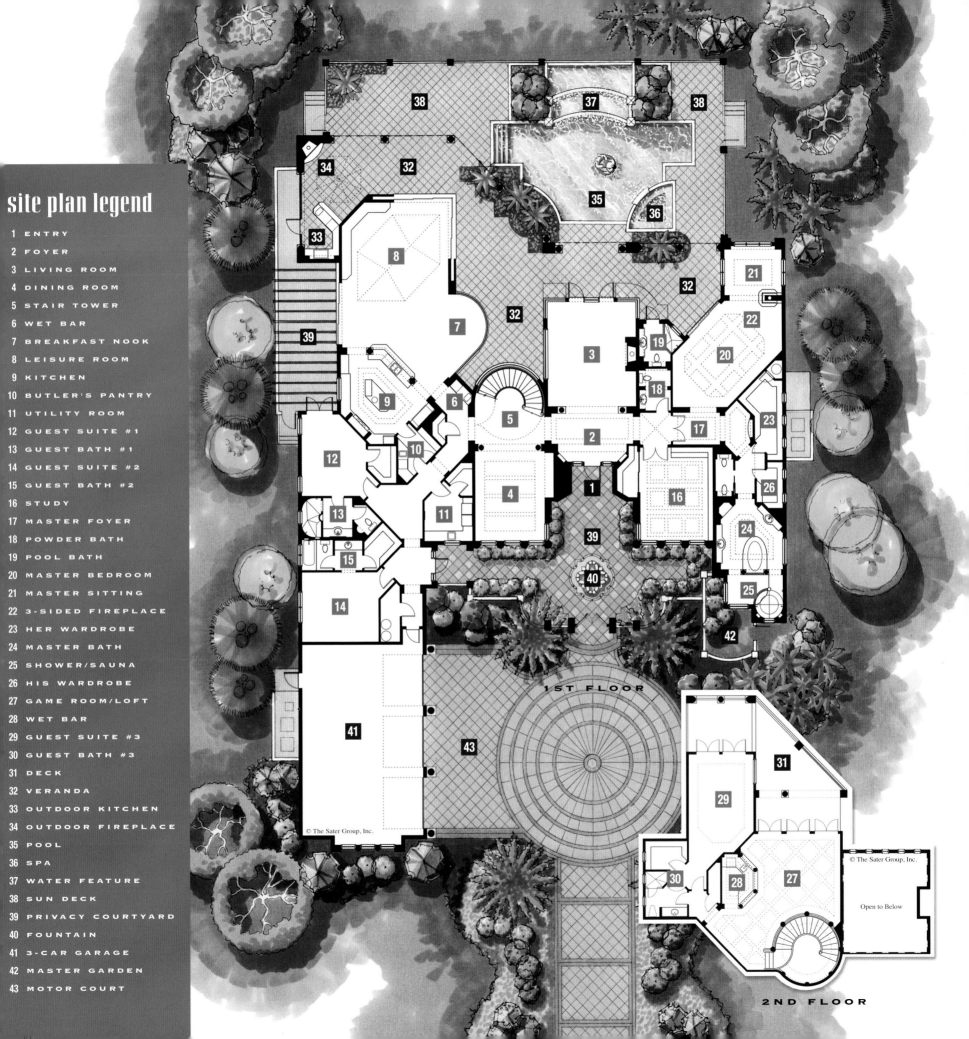

site plan legend

1 ENTRY
2 FOYER
3 LIVING ROOM
4 DINING ROOM
5 STAIR TOWER
6 WET BAR
7 BREAKFAST NOOK
8 LEISURE ROOM
9 KITCHEN
10 BUTLER'S PANTRY
11 UTILITY ROOM
12 GUEST SUITE #1
13 GUEST BATH #1
14 GUEST SUITE #2
15 GUEST BATH #2
16 STUDY
17 MASTER FOYER
18 POWDER BATH
19 POOL BATH
20 MASTER BEDROOM
21 MASTER SITTING
22 3-SIDED FIREPLACE
23 HER WARDROBE
24 MASTER BATH
25 SHOWER/SAUNA
26 HIS WARDROBE
27 GAME ROOM/LOFT
28 WET BAR
29 GUEST SUITE #3
30 GUEST BATH #3
31 DECK
32 VERANDA
33 OUTDOOR KITCHEN
34 OUTDOOR FIREPLACE
35 POOL
36 SPA
37 WATER FEATURE
38 SUN DECK
39 PRIVACY COURTYARD
40 FOUNTAIN
41 3-CAR GARAGE
42 MASTER GARDEN
43 MOTOR COURT

1ST FLOOR

© The Sater Group, Inc.

Open to Below

© The Sater Group, Inc.

2ND FLOOR

Pietra Mar

© THE SATER GROUP, INC.

Casual living and elegant style come together in this island retreat.

dan's notes | *The clients had a very specific vision for this home that included large, comfortable spaces for their guests and family. I knew they wanted a tropical getaway and a sense of informality, and that the site— on a stretch of coastline along the Gulf of Mexico— would offer spectacular views. So I drew what basically became an extended L-shaped plan, keeping the landscape in mind. There is grandeur about this plan, yet the house easily takes in scenery, and the courtyard, loggia, terrace and decks expand the living areas into the outdoors.*

Located on Sanibel Island with rear views oriented toward the Gulf of Mexico, the house enjoys an informal elegance that prevails throughout its open interior. Flow and function are intimately connected in the plan, with easy transitions between public and private realms. Fluid spaces defined by views of the water framed with groves of Gumbo Limbo trees enhance the sense of openness. Casual and formal rooms flex to accommodate family gatherings and planned events, and mitered windows and sliding doors provide links to the lanai. On the upper level, a luxurious retreat dedicated to the private use of the owners includes an observation deck and a glass sitting bay with panoramic views of the Gulf.

LOCATION:
SANIBEL ISLAND, FLORIDA

BUILDER: THE WOLTER GROUP

LANDSCAPE ARCHITECT:
SMALLWOOD DESIGN GROUP
SCOTT WINDHAM, ASLA

INTERIOR DESIGN:
MARC MICHAELS INTERIORS

PHOTOGRAPHY BY:
LAURENCE TAYLOR

PIETRA MAR

entry foyer | A series of graceful arches—supported by massive, floor-to-ceiling columns—frame the gallery linking the foyer and entry to a spacious guest suite. Rows of radius windows line the stairwell, revealing glimpses of the entry porch and subtropical scenery.

grand room | Open to the foyer, the grand room offers an inviting ambience for guests, with wrapping walls of glass that reveal breathtaking panoramas of the sea. The cove ceiling enhances the visual dimensions of the room, and a large fanlight transom highlights a set of glass doors that lead to the lanai. A row of sculpted arches permits spatial intimacy between the grand room and media room, which provides an informal gathering area and home entertainment center.

wine cellar | A richly carved, drop-leaf tasting
table serves both function and form in the wine room,
which is designed to maintain the owners' vintage
collection at a constant temperature. Located near the
kitchen, the wine cellar adjoins the butler's pantry,
which eases the service for traditional occasions.

dining room | Marble floors unify the grand room
with the formal dining room, enhanced by two graceful
stucco archways that help to define the individuality of
the spaces. The carved Crema Maya surround lends
texture to the room and enlivens a masonry fireplace
shared by the two rooms. Views of the Gulf of Mexico
mingle with refined elements of the public realm,
creating a relaxed yet elegant environment.

master bedroom | The magnificent upper-level master suite is embraced by views brought in by a series of windows surrounding the sitting bay. To the left, a set of French doors lead to an observation deck oriented toward the Gulf.

master bath | A radius-beamed, sloped ceiling highlights the master bath, which permits plenty of natural light through a series of ribbon windows. The rugged stone-and-marble tub surround iterates the casually elegant scheme of the home.

kitchen | In the gourmet kitchen, paneled
European cabinetry sets off stone tile floors
that help to unify the palette. A food-preparation island complements the service area,
while a butler's pantry provides culinary space
for planned events. The pass-through links the
kitchen with the formal dining room.

rear balcony | Surrounded by views of Sanibel Island, the observation deck overlooks a series of stairs leading down to the beach. Carved balusters cantilever above the lanai, and lead to the pool and spa area. A graceful arcade frames the deck and offers shelter from the midday sun.

pool view | An elevated deck harbors the spa at the rear of the home, surrounded by a luxe pool complete with water features, stepping stones and subtropical landscaping. Wrapped by a portico, the upper level overlooks the outdoor zone. A balustrade lining the stairs to the lower pool area echoes the linear motion of the perimeter.

Pietra Mar | SATER TODAY

site plan legend

1 ENTRY
2 FOYER
3 STUDY
4 DINING ROOM
5 KITCHEN
6 NOOK
7 GRAND ROOM
8 MEDIA
9 GUEST BEDROOM #1
10 GUEST BATH #1
11 GUEST LIVING
12 GUEST BEDROOM #2
13 GUEST BATH #2
14 GUEST BEDROOM #3
15 GUEST BATH #3
16 GUEST BEDROOM #4
17 GUEST BATH #4
18 MASTER FOYER
19 MASTER SUITE
20 MASTER BATH
21 HER WARDROBE
22 HIS WARDROBE
23 LIBRARY/LOFT
24 POWDER BATH
25 UTILITY
26 GALLERY
27 BREEZEWAY
28 LANAI
29 DECK
30 OUTDOOR KITCHEN
31 OBSERVATION DECK
32 SPA
33 POOL
34 ENTRY PORCH
35 MOTOR COURT

LOWER LEVEL:
TWO 2-CAR GARAGES
ELEVATOR
STORAGE

rear view | A winding staircase leads down from the extensive loggia to the pool and spa arena. Graceful arcades line the perimeter of the home, echoing the curvature of the main gable and Palladian-style arch. Deeply recessed rooflines help to protect the sitting areas and provide shelter from the sun's harsh rays. To the left, an observation deck with a wide-open view of the sea offers a secluded area and a sensational spa.

site plan | Announced by a grand stairway, the formal entry leads to an open arena comprised of the grand room, foyer and formal dining room. Along the rear perimeter, a wall of glass permits wide views of the Gulf of Mexico, and access to the lanai through sets of sliding doors. A beamed ceiling highlights a secluded study bordered by a curved wall of glass that visually links the space with the outdoors. A rambling upper-level master suite, library and loft complement four guest suites on the main floor.

© The Sater Group, Inc.

The Sater Group, Inc.

31

19

21

23 18

20

22

2ND FLOOR

33

32

28

28

28

30

6

5

7

8

4

3

26

2

26

14

16

34

24

15

17

1

26

13

25

12

1ST FLOOR

27

11

10

9

35

29

Malya

©THE SATER GROUP, INC.

Villa-by-the-sea creates harmony with the past and present.

dan's notes | *Our clients chose an authentic Tuscan architectural style for their home, so I wanted to bring in evocative elements—such as carved limestone, mahogany trim and Ludowici clay roof tiles—that would also fit the coastal site. The solid-rail balconies, massive stone gables, carved-wood corbels and recessed entry are programmatic essentials that provide a sense of history. I developed the fractured vertical scale at the streetscape to lend a sense of layering over time and to prevent the house from appearing too large. Trees from the front courtyard actually peek above the entry surround to accentuate the stepped-back massing and enhance the secluded approach to the entry.*

Prior to breaking ground, the owners made clear their desire for an Old World villa-by-the-sea approach to a narrow, elongated waterfront site. Natural growth frames the edges of the stone pavers leading to the wrought-iron entry gates, which link to the front courtyard. A mosaic tile centerpiece anchors the front terrace, with planters and tall trees at each corner flanking sets of French doors that access separate guest wings and bring in natural light. The formal dining room enjoys a vista of the entry court as well as the Gulf through a wall of windows in the grand salon. French doors lead to a sun deck and down to the sea via the poolside steps.

LOCATION:
MARCO ISLAND, FLORIDA

BUILDER:
SNELL CONSTRUCTION

LANDSCAPE ARCHITECT:
OUTSIDE PRODUCTIONS, INC.

INTERIOR DESIGN: DAVID L. SMITH
INTERIORS, GARY CLARK

PHOTOGRAPHY BY:
CJ WALKER

179

front view | Rough-hewn pavers unify the approach to the formal entry, framed by massive twin gables that harbor the plan's two guest suites. Cypress trees imported from California set off an enchanting façade clad in New Mexican limestone. Corbels line a Ludowici clay-tile roof, while traditional stone quoins reinforce the upper decks and entry.

rear view | Stone steps lead past the terrace to the rear entry and grand salon—an interior space that enjoys Gulf views—which leads to a sun deck. On the lower level, French doors open directly to the pool, allowing the owners to step into the water from the casual living zone. A limestone-clad veranda harbors an alfresco dining area, defined by a colonnade that serves as a fountain, with waterspouts directed to the pool.

Malya | SATER TODAY

rear view | Tall symmetrical windows sentinel the inviting retreat at the rear of the home, which includes a sun deck with poolside seating. The rear elevation embraces the lush scenery and airy feel of its exuberant seaside location.

site plan | High above the water, the upper-level plan offers unobstructed views of the horizon. Dedicated to the owners' private realm, the floor offers a shared sleeping and sitting space and independent amenities, including "his and hers" studies, dressing areas and baths. The main level

wraps an interior courtyard with two guest wings that provide individual entries off the foyer. A vantage point for views of the Gulf, the central dining room opens to the spacious grand salon. A winding stair tower links the lower-level garage to a rooftop deck with a 360-degree view of the sea.

site plan legend

1 GROUND LEVEL ENTRY
2 GROUND LEVEL FOYER
3 GRAND SALON
4 HER STUDY
5 HIS STUDY
6 DINING ROOM
7 HER BATH
8 HIS BATH
9 MASTER SUITE
10 MASTER SITTING
11 MASTER FOYER
12 HER WARDROBE
13 HIS WARDROBE
14 A.M. KITCHEN
15 POWDER BATH
16 NOOK
17 KITCHEN
18 SUN DECK
19 POOL
20 UTILITY ROOM
21 BALCONY
22 GUEST SUITE #1
23 GUEST BATH #1
24 GUEST SUITE #2
25 GUEST BATH #2
26 GALLERY
27 SPA
28 FIREPLACE
29 STORAGE
30 ELEVATOR
31 COURTYARD
32 POOL DECK

GROUND LEVEL:
TWO 2-CAR GARAGES
MEDIA ROOM
GAME ROOM

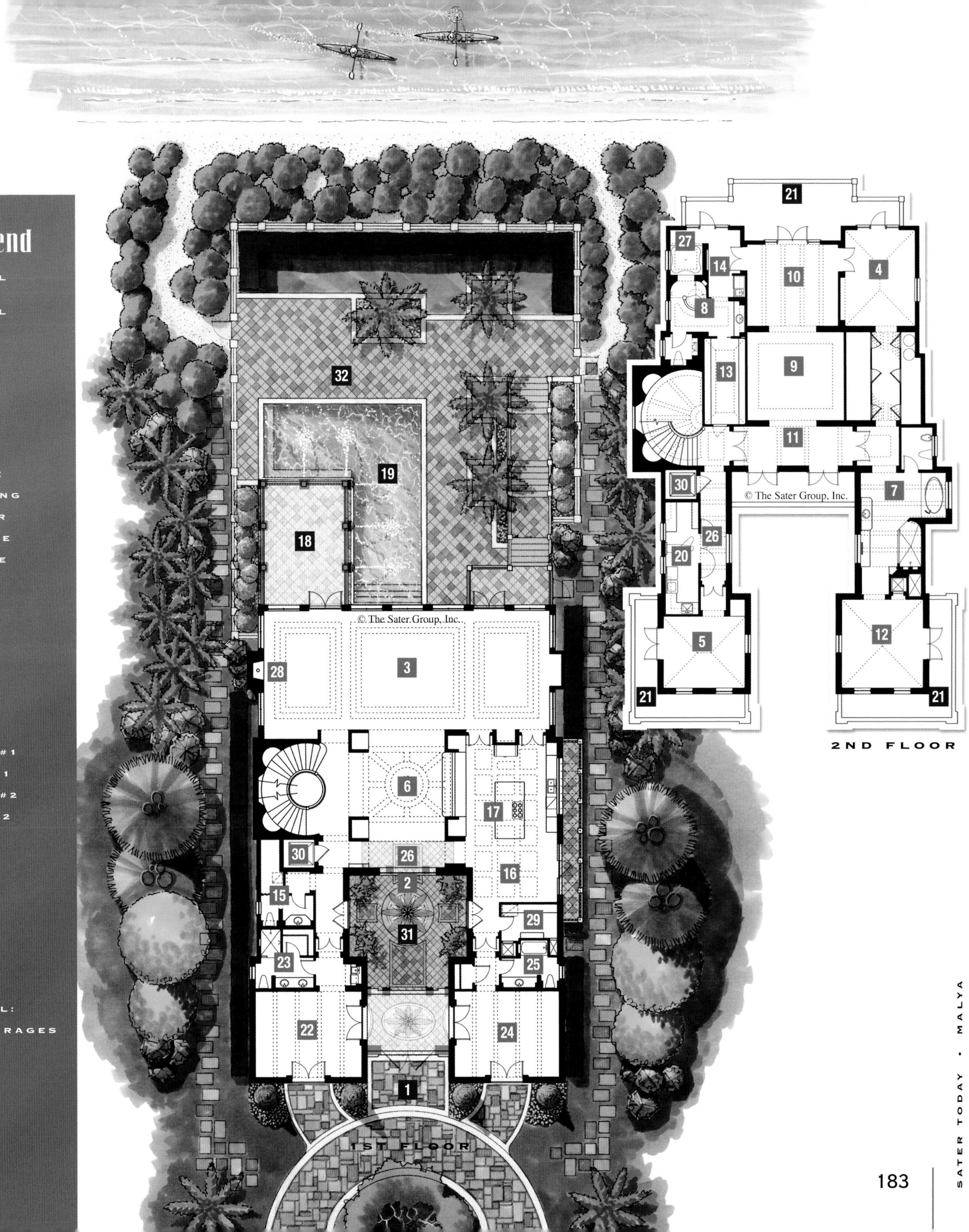

© The Sater Group, Inc.

© The Sater Group, Inc.

2ND FLOOR

1ST FLOOR

SATER TODAY · MALYA

183

Villoresi

© THE SATER GROUP, INC.

Courtyard home transforms European revival architecture.

dan's notes | *Set into a tight coastal lot, this European-style plan required lateral dimensions suitably scaled to the narrow approach, with vertical massing that would allow a variety of views. A central courtyard creates a sense of openness and brings an outdoor experience into the home. In many ways, it is a regional home—with informal elements such as the cabana and club room—yet the clients' need for traditional space led to the design of the grand salon, which has a refined, classical tone. The wrapping loggia parallels the interior gallery, connecting the interior to the outer spaces—an arrangement that unifies the plan.*

A mere stone's throw from the Gulf of Mexico and nestled beside a live oak grove and wetlands preserve, this courtyard villa conforms to an unusual triangular site, with a curved driveway defining its inland edges. Paired balconies address the eastern streetscape with a playful elegance that sets the theme of the home, enlivened by a well-scaled tower and porte-cochere. Elevated one level up, the front entry confronts tradition with an arrangement of gables layered inward toward the bay. The Tuscan-yellow stucco and clay-tile roof suggest the plan's Italian Country provenance, yet the house exhibits a satisfying mix of architectural influences. Hispanic elements, such as the multi-level roof, double-sash doors and wrought-iron balconies, lend eclectic qualities to the home, while a main-level gallery exhibits a purely colonial disposition. The courtyard enlarges the sense of light and space within the home by extending the sight lines.

LOCATION: MARCO ISLAND, FLORIDA

BUILDER: SNELL CONSTRUCTION

LANDSCAPE ARCHITECT:
OUTSIDE PRODUCTIONS, INC.
SCOTT WINDHAM, ASLA

INTERIOR DESIGN:
DAVID L. SMITH INTERIORS

PHOTOGRAPHY BY: CJ WALKER

stair entry |

Unlike houses inland, this Gulf Coast home requires a minimum above-ground elevation due to regional regulations. Scaled to the traditions and pedestrian standards of the neighborhood, the plan employs a shapely balustrade to animate the façade and visually connect the formal entry to the street-level porte-cochere. With turn-of-the-century grandeur, the staircase exhibits the carefree nature of a home by the sea with a playful, sweeping curve.

spiral stair view |

Limestone stairs wind up the primary tower of the elevation from the foyer to the private vestibule of the master retreat. At the top level, a carved edge of the landing cantilevers over the ordered pattern of steps. Viewed from above, the solid-maple railing creates a ripple of convex curves.

nook balcony |

A trio of French doors leads from the morning nook to a wrapping balcony that overlooks the forward property. Just to the left of the porte-cochere, the layered massing of the elevation is repeated at the upper-level bay that harbors "her" study.

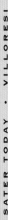

courtyard pool | Crisp, rectilinear lines frame the splendid courtyard placed at the center of the home's lateral wings. Roman Doric columns and sculpted arches border the rear perimeter and harbor a sea-blue pool oriented toward the Gulf of Mexico. To the left of the upper portico, top gables recede from the roofline, adding a layered texture to the elevation. The trellis above the seating area provides shelter from the sun's rays.

kitchen | Muted walls and earthy hues create an appropriate foundation for an idyllic beachside palette in a space surrounded by views and sunlight from the bay nook. Glossy painted trim enriches paneled cabinetry and sand-colored granite counters.

his study | The upper-level gallery leads to the husband's private retreat: an area used primarily for business yet also for reading and casual conversation. Deeply paneled cabinetry and bold leather furnishings form classic embellishments in a room laden with texture. An ebonized coffered ceiling offsets an amber hardwood floor with French doors leading out to a secluded balcony.

main foyer and stairs | The grand foyer harbors an inviting transitional space that leads into the home in several directions. An arched passageway connects the grand salon to a gallery stretching the width of the courtyard. Limestone stairs sweep through the turret, linking the main-level living areas to the master and guest suites.

dining room | Rows of glass doors open the formal dining room to the wide courtyard and more intimate loggia. Views pour in through a series of radius windows that line this space and the gallery leading back to the foyer. A splendid coffered ceiling adds depth to the airy dimensions of the room, ennobled by shapely carved wood furnishings and a vintage chandelier.

ante room/gallery | Lava-grey and bianco stone tiles create a classic checkerboard pattern on the floor of the gallery. Imagined as an exhibit hall for the owners' valuable art collection, the passage permits plenty of natural light to illumine the displays. The ultra-linear dimensions of the space are transformed by sets of glass doors leading out to the courtyard.

living room |
Infused with sunlight, the grand salon overlooks a large wetlands preserve—a view that contributes to the relaxed environment of the formal living space—and opens to a balcony. To the left, a second series of glass doors brings in more light and leads out to the courtyard. Striped fauteuils oppose a grouping of plush chenille sofas and sable-upholstered bergères around a mahogany fireplace that serves as a focal point. Twin archways framing the rear wall offer links to a secluded club room with Gulf views.

courtyard loggia |
Oriented to the coast, the loggia offers views of the Gulf of Mexico through the courtyard, the home's most scenic outdoor living area. A majestic counterpart to the interior gallery, the groin-vaulted colonnade links the traditional living spaces—the formal dining room and grand salon—without restrictions to scenery and fresh air. Low-key elegance defines the alcove and alfresco seating, creating a sense of shelter and utilizing a series of massive columns and vaulted arches to align views. Beyond the dining room, the wrapping loggia connects to an outdoor kitchen, cabana and nook.

Villoresi | SATER TODAY

courtyard deck | With the air of a Mediterranean villa, the rear elevation wraps the pool area and courtyard with a splendid colonnade and upper deck. A detailed wrought-iron balustrade and ochre-washed stucco create an authentic marriage of Old World elements and modern architectural forms. To the right, an extension of the tile roof shelters an outdoor fireplace and living area. At the end of the guest wing, a bay cantilevers above a poolside retreat, and a private deck offers respite for the travel-weary.

site plan | On an angular site, this house takes its cues from the landscape and grants views in every direction. Elevated to conform to the slope, the plan allows parking and storage below the main level. A central courtyard increases circulation and infuses the interior with daylight. Formal rooms linked by a gallery open to outdoor living spaces, including an alfresco kitchen, cabana and bay, taking in views of the Gulf. On the upper level, a sun deck wraps the master retreat and guest suites with a sense of nature.

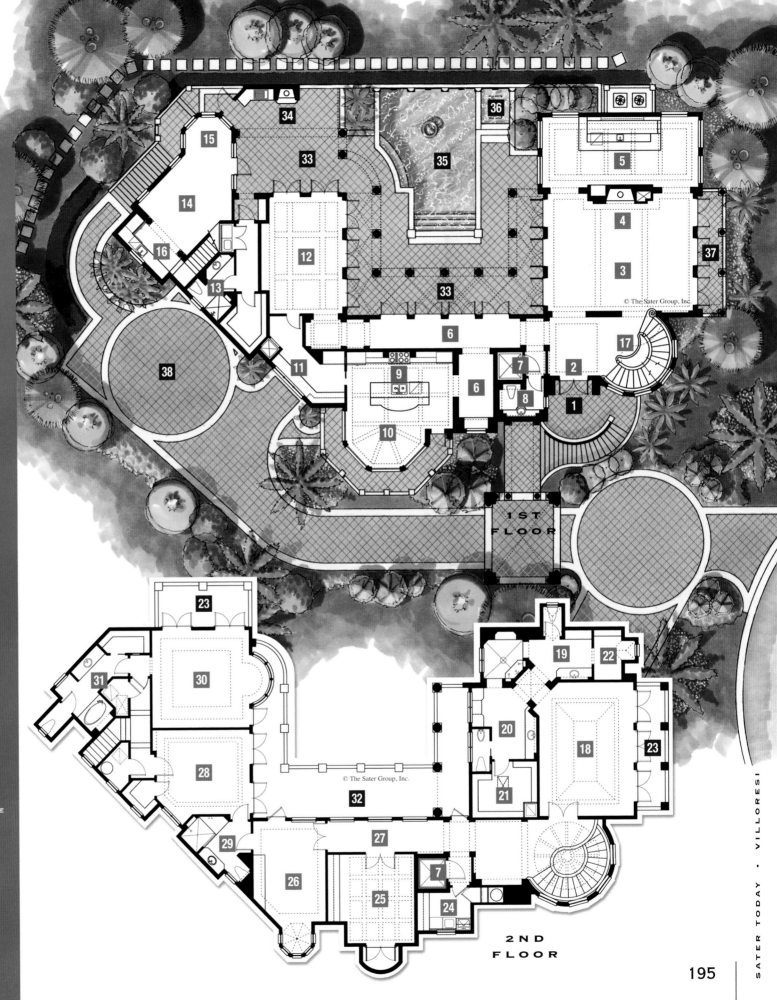

site plan legend

1 ENTRY
2 FOYER
3 GRAND SALON
4 FIREPLACE
5 CLUB ROOM
6 ANTE ROOM
7 ELEVATOR
8 POWDER BATH
9 KITCHEN
10 BREAKFAST NOOK
11 BUTLER'S PANTRY
12 DINING ROOM
13 POOL BATH
14 CABANA
15 NOOK
16 WET BAR
17 STAIR TOWER
18 MASTER SUITE
19 HIS BATH
20 HER BATH
21 HER WARDROBE
22 HIS WARDROBE
23 BALCONY
24 UTILITY ROOM
25 HIS STUDY
26 HER STUDY
27 GALLERY
28 GUEST SUITE #1
29 GUEST BATH #1
30 GUEST SUITE #2
31 GUEST BATH #2
32 SUN DECK
33 LOGGIA
34 OUTDOOR FIREPLACE
35 POOL
36 SPA
37 BALCONY
38 MOTOR COURT

LOWER LEVEL:
FOYER
ELEVATOR
1 & 2-CAR GARAGES

1ST FLOOR

2ND FLOOR

© The Sater Group, Inc.

Fiorentino

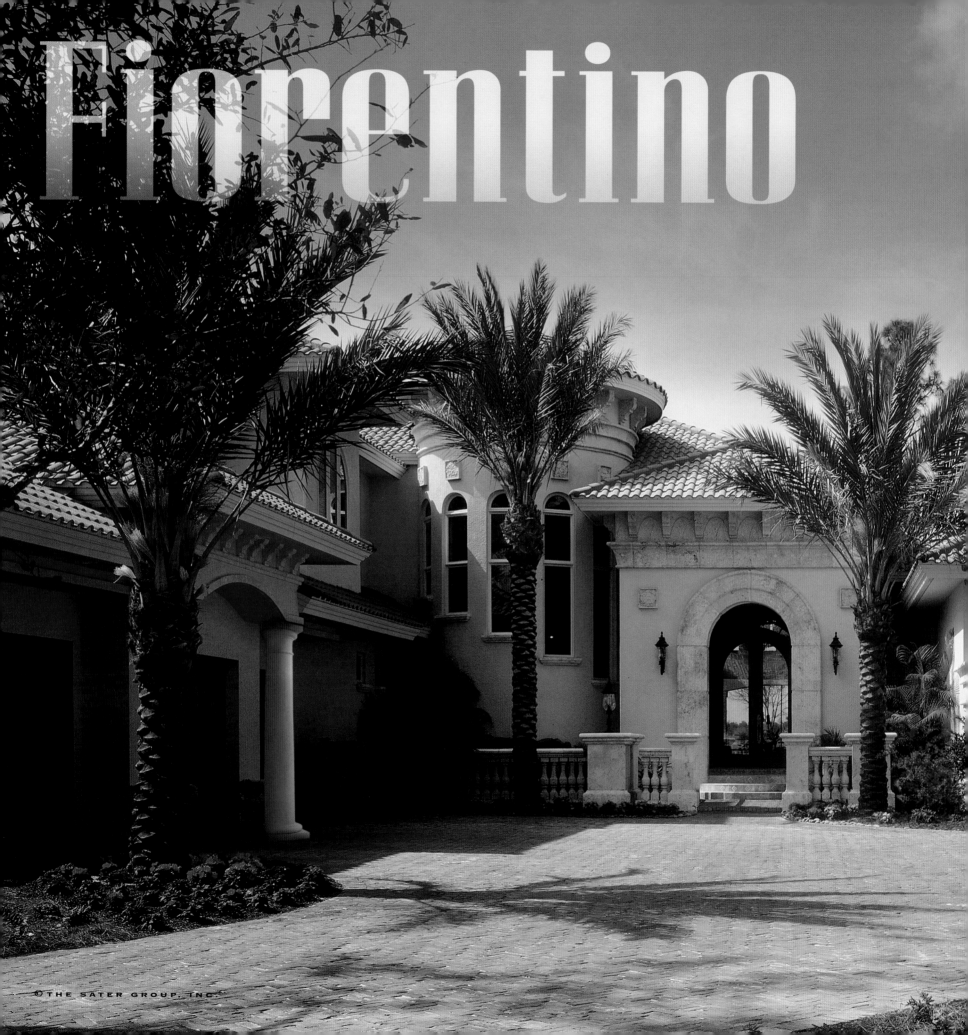

©THE SATER GROUP, INC.

Prize-winning retreat offers serenity and comfort.

dan's notes | *This formal design is rich with Old World details and features a courtyard approach and stately surround at the entry. Water elements at the front of the home and beyond the rear wall add an interactive dimension to the design, creating a sense of movement and connection to the environment. The façade makes a grand statement that continues through the plan with many dramatic elements, such as the vaulted glass windows and retreating walls. Coffered ceilings with carved radius beams and sculpted arches add depth to the home, and layered massing contributes a Tuscan influence.*

High-volume ceilings, picturesque arcades and graceful arches were carefully designed to enhance the lakeside vistas that surround this Mediterranean home. Winner of the AIBD's 2001 Designer's Choice Award, the plan features authentic Old World themes that relate well to modern aesthetics and 21st-century functions. Carved-wood panels, intricate wrought-iron railings, and rich marble floors complement the courtyard feel of the home, and engage vistas defined by flowing forms and open boundaries. Organic architecture links refined spaces to one another using vistas and archways, creating harmonious relationships and intimacy with the outdoors. On the upper level, the loft visually connects a guest wing, billiard room and landing with the formal realm below.

LOCATION: NAPLES, FLORIDA

BUILDER:
HARBOURSIDE CUSTOM HOMES

LANDSCAPE ARCHITECT:
OUTSIDE PRODUCTIONS, INC.

INTERIOR DESIGN:
FREESTYLE INTERIORS

PHOTOGRAPHY BY: DAN FORER

living room |

A rotunda ceiling defines the circular dimensions of the heart of the home. The space is surrounded by alcoves, and columns define passage to the formal dining room. An integral part of the function and flow of the home, the living room animates the public realm and serves as a hub of circulation to the opposing wings as well as the loggia. A trio of transom windows lends an ecclesiastical layer to a refined scheme that is repeated throughout the home, even in the private retreats.

breakfast nook |

Wide mitered windows express the intimate connections the home shares with the outdoors, and visually extend the casual living spaces to the loggia. Outdoor sitting and eating areas employ the arcade to provide shelter from the sun.

entry foyer/stairs |

Carved-wood beams and a vintage medallion soar above the vaulted spaces of the entry hall, emphasizing the dramatic scheme of the home. An open arrangement of the forward rooms permits natural light and views to penetrate the formal core of the plan, enriched by a series of stepped windows at the entry that follow the ascending line of the stairs. Just below the foyer level, the wine cellar lends depth and dimension to the gallery, and links spatially to the opposing wet bar.

Fiorentino | SATER TODAY

rear pool view | Views into the casual living area from the rear property reveal an inviting and well-lived-in home, with easy transitions between rooms. Retreating glass walls bring in a sense of nature to the leisure room and extend its boundaries to the outdoors.

master bath | Crema Marfil marble tile surrounds the step-up tub in the owners' private bath. A trio of windows permits glimpses of a privacy garden surrounding the bay.

site plan | A contemporary layout positions rooms side-by-side in an open arrangement that eases the flow and function of the whole house. Views extend past the fountain, pool and spa to a lake and fairway, filling the home with a sense of nature. Guest suites are designed for visits from family members, positioned for privacy and access to outside environments. The loft offers flexible space that extends to an impressive deck and game room. French doors on both levels lead to outside living spaces and, in the leisure room, retreating glass walls create an intimate connection with the loggia.

200

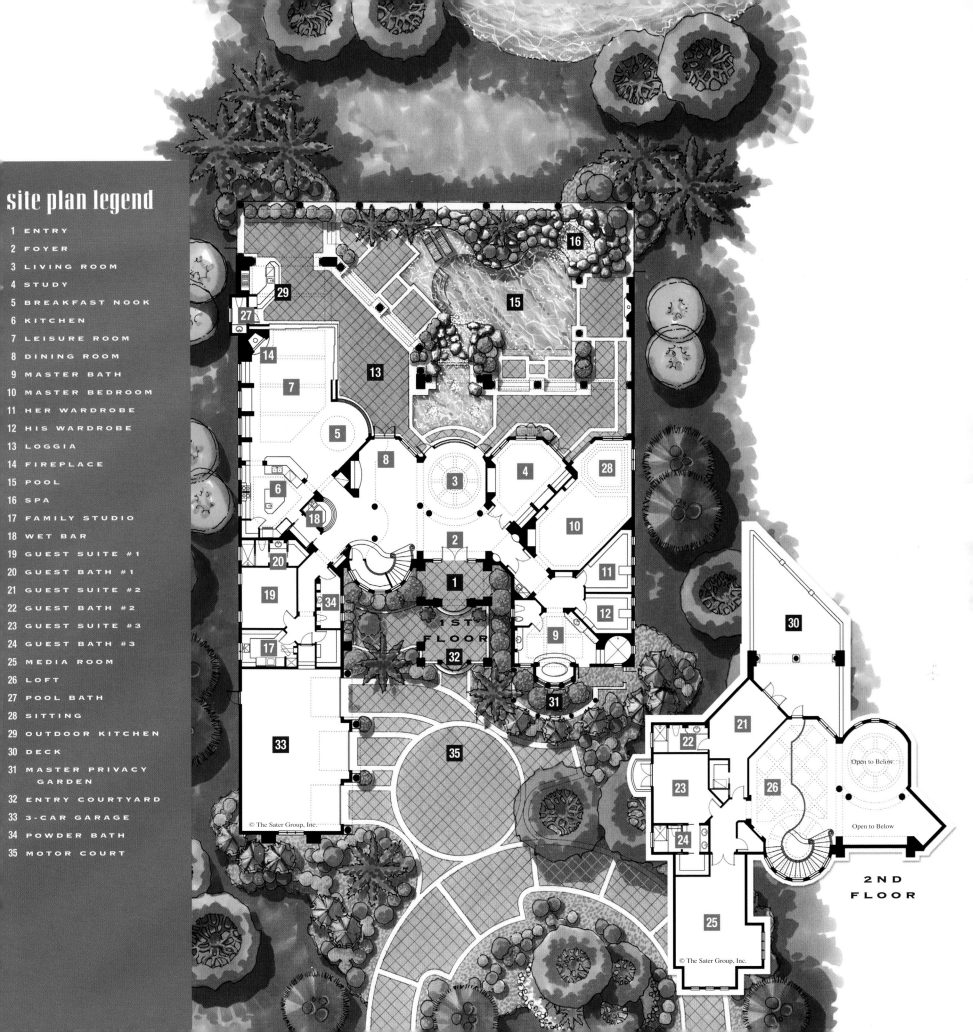

site plan legend

1 ENTRY
2 FOYER
3 LIVING ROOM
4 STUDY
5 BREAKFAST NOOK
6 KITCHEN
7 LEISURE ROOM
8 DINING ROOM
9 MASTER BATH
10 MASTER BEDROOM
11 HER WARDROBE
12 HIS WARDROBE
13 LOGGIA
14 FIREPLACE
15 POOL
16 SPA
17 FAMILY STUDIO
18 WET BAR
19 GUEST SUITE #1
20 GUEST BATH #1
21 GUEST SUITE #2
22 GUEST BATH #2
23 GUEST SUITE #3
24 GUEST BATH #3
25 MEDIA ROOM
26 LOFT
27 POOL BATH
28 SITTING
29 OUTDOOR KITCHEN
30 DECK
31 MASTER PRIVACY
   GARDEN
32 ENTRY COURTYARD
33 3-CAR GARAGE
34 POWDER BATH
35 MOTOR COURT

1ST FLOOR

2ND FLOOR

Open to Below

Open to Below

© The Sater Group, Inc.

© The Sater Group, Inc.

Alamosa

©THE SATER GROUP, INC.

European disposition inspires a sense of place.

dan's notes | *Pre-classical elements and large-scale architectural treatments contribute to the grand, Old World character of this plan. Based in part on my admiration for original Italian styles, the house makes a claim on the past—yet I designed the rooms to relate to one another and flow easily into the outside spaces. In the casual area, retreating walls allow an easy transition to the loggia. In other places—such as the master wing—the relationship to the lanai, solana and pool is more subtle, through a series of French doors.*

Stone accents, hipped rooflines and stucco surrounds evoke a 16th-century Italian vocabulary with this Mediterranean villa. A broad square cupola and overhanging eaves reveal an early influence, with a traditional forecourt leading to the formal entry. Soaring coffered and curved beamed ceilings define the open boundaries of the public rooms, framed by a rib-vaulted arcade lined with massive pre-classical marble columns. Natural materials enrich an open interior, designed to extend its visual boundaries to the outdoors throughout the home. The entry, foyer and core living areas are axially related to opposing wings, linked by a gallery hall. Guest suites enjoy access to outdoor amenities, and a rambling master suite features a garden bath.

LOCATION: NAPLES, FLORIDA

BUILDER:
HARBOURSIDE CUSTOM HOMES

LANDSCAPE ARCHITECT:
OUTSIDE PRODUCTIONS, INC.
PAT TREFZ, ASLA

INTERIOR DESIGN: VOGUE INTERIORS,
DEBBIE DI MARIA

PHOTOGRAPHY BY:
MICHAEL LOWRY

family room/kitchen | Stone floors and
coffered ceilings define the wide-open spaces of the
casual living area. Terracotta-hued mosaic tiles and
paneled cabinetry lend an inviting Old World character
to the kitchen. An arching doorway secludes a conven-
ient butler's pantry that links the food-preparation
area to a wet bar and wine cellar. Varied architectural
forms give shape to this multi-function space, with
columns and sculpted arches connecting the rooms,
and to a curved vestibule leading to the main gallery.

living room exterior | Classical forms frame
the central living room, harbored by a bow window.
A beamed ceiling accentuates the curvilinear struc-
tures surrounding the space: the grand entry, a series
of arched transoms and the exterior arcade flanking
the pool. Overhanging eaves supported by decorative
brackets indicate the plan's renaissance roots. A three-
point fountain offers a soothing vista to the formal
interior, and provides a water feature that flows into
the main pool.

foyer/grand solana | Carved Crema Maya

stone columns articulate the boundaries of the formal dining room, enhanced by a barrel-vaulted ceiling. The cupola shelters a sitting space in front of the fireplace, while ornate floriated capitals repeat the classical patterns of the surround and frieze. A vintage chandelier sets off a circular sofa that takes full advantage of the warmth radiated from an ornately carved two-story fireplace. Views extend from the foyer to the rear property through a bow window in the living room, while French doors extend the dining area to an outdoor space.

solana | Laden in stone, the *plein air* solana
extends the livability of the leisure room and includes
a corner fireplace and an alfresco kitchen. Cypress
planks line the ceiling of the outdoor zone, providing
definition to the space, set off by recessed lighting and
a wrought-iron chandelier. A neo-chromatic scheme
employs varied textures to enrich the setting, with
furnishings of wicker, wood and stone. Encircled by a
grand arcade, the outer living and dining areas are
closely linked to the pool, fountain and spa by a
curving walkway that leads to dual lanais. Retreating
glass doors dissolve boundaries of indoors and out at
the perimeter of the leisure room.

dining room | The curved beams of the barrel-vaulted ceiling in the formal dining room are brought into high relief by panels of deep sienna. An interior wall provides an ample canvas for a muted *trompe l'oeil* that deepens the dimensions of the room and lends a sense of tradition to the public realm. Massive columns of a pre-classical order anchor the boundaries of the room and evoke ancient themes.

master bedroom | A series of square transoms and a stunning mitered-glass window set off the sitting bay of the owners' suite, permitting views and light to enhance the retreat. Soaring ceiling coffers contrast with the linear forms of the space, and heighten the visual dimensions of the room. French doors lead to the pool and spa and a private lanai with views that extend beyond the property.

Alamosa | SATER TODAY

rear view | Open rooms engage the rear perimeter of the home with wide views and a sense of the outdoors. A double portico shapes the vaulted solana and provides a frame for balconies that lead to upper-level retreats. French doors seclude a guest suite above the outdoor living zone and glass walls allow natural light to permeate the leisure room from the top floor. A series of stepped and square transoms, sculpted arches and curvilinear forms lend depth to the layered elevation.

site plan | Built around a forecourt, the forward plan offers a gracious welcome to the formal entry. The foyer and grand salon—an open arena with views to the fountain and pool—encircle a space sheltered by the cupola, and warmed by a stone fireplace. A vestibule harboring a wine cellar serves as a terminus to the central gallery and leads to the casual living area. The upper level features a loft with links to the media room, sun deck, exercise room and a spacious guest suite.

site plan legend

1 ENTRY
2 FOYER
3 GRAND SOLANA
4 STUDY
5 DINING ROOM
6 GALLERY
7 NOOK
8 LEISURE ROOM
9 KITCHEN
10 WET BAR
11 POWDER BATH
12 WINE CELLAR
13 MASTER SUITE
14 MASTER BATH
15 MASTER SITTING
16 MASTER WARDROBE
17 MORNING KITCHEN
18 GUEST SUITE #1
19 GUEST BATH #1
20 GUEST SUITE #2
21 GUEST BATH #2
22 GUEST SUITE #3
23 GUEST BATH #3
24 GUEST SUITE #4
25 GUEST BATH #4
26 UTILITY
27 MEDIA ROOM
28 LOFT
29 EXERCISE ROOM
30 2-SIDED FIREPLACE
31 OUTDOOR KITCHEN
32 SOLANA
33 OUTDOOR FIREPLACE
34 LANAI
35 MASTER GARDEN
36 BALCONY
37 SIDE COURTYARD
38 POOL
39 SPA
40 3-CAR GARAGE
41 ELEVATOR
42 MOTOR COURT

1ST FLOOR

2ND FLOOR

Open to Cupola Above

Open to Below

© The Sater Group, Inc.

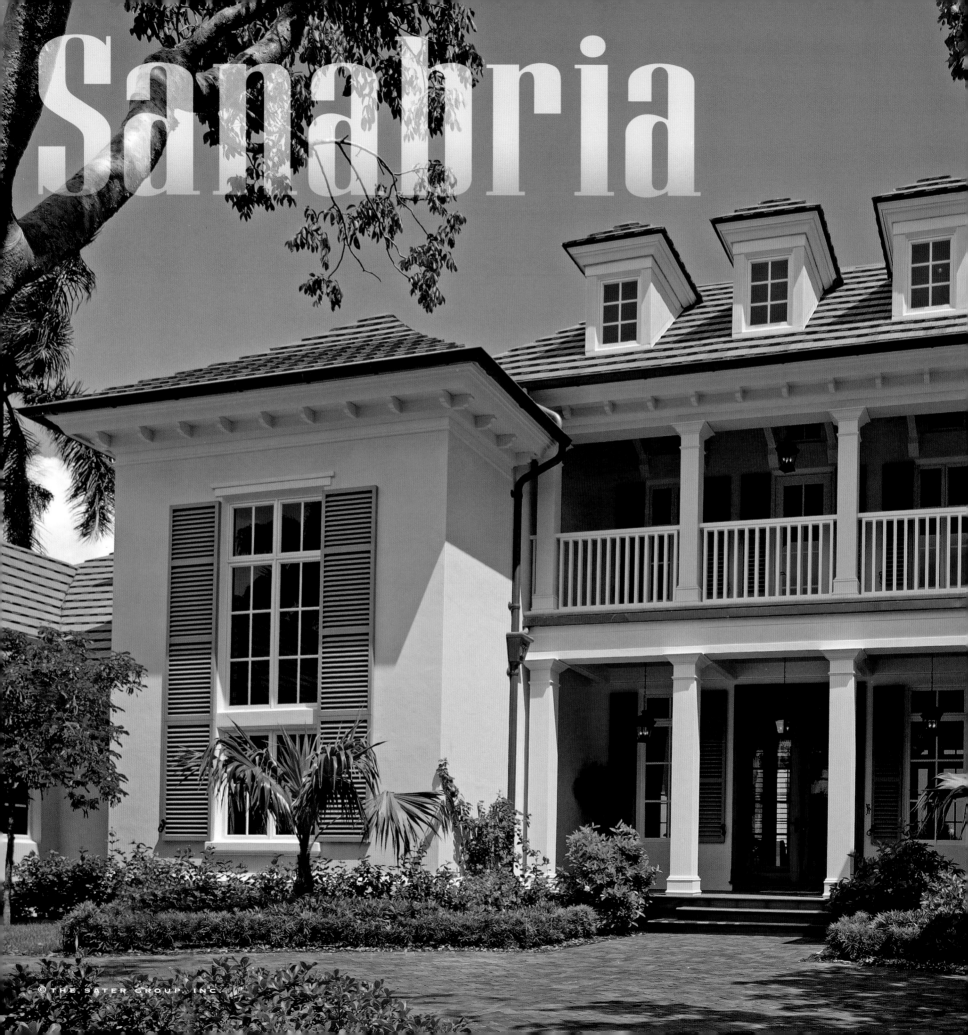

Sanabria

© THE SATER GROUP, INC.

Colonial coastal manor embraces views of the sea.

dan's notes | *This elegant home with waterfront views of Keewaydin and Gordon's Pass holds strong links to the outdoors with a wrapping veranda, private pier and dock for the owners' yacht. The architecture is drawn from the simple, very formal, manor and plantation houses of the region, yet the home is designed for a casual lifestyle. This is a getaway retreat for the clients, and I wanted the rooms to be visually connected to the sea. I drew the main living areas to merge fluidly with the outdoor spaces. For example, the study and parlor open on both sides to the outdoors, allowing cross breezes to fill the home on each level.*

Located on a beachfront lot on Gordon's Pass—a mere 500 yards from the Gulf of Mexico—this Floridian retreat evokes the elegance and orchestrated charm of the French Colonial and Caribbean-style houses that dominated the region during the 19th and early 20th centuries. Wide porches and hipped roofs—freely adapted from Colonial Revival styles—satisfy the waterfront neighborhood's affinity for classic forms and contribute to an intimate link to the locale. True to its provenance, the house lives outward, with all of the main living spaces connected to the open-air galleries, such as the veranda, lanai and solana. The linear architecture aligns the opposing wings along a horizontal axis, and expresses the formality of the home.

LOCATION: NAPLES, FLORIDA

BUILDER: KURTZ HOMES

LANDSCAPE ARCHITECT:
RUSSELL P. BENCAZ & ASSOCIATES, INC.

INTERIOR DESIGN: NANCY RUZICKA

PHOTOGRAPHY BY: CJ WALKER

entry parlor |

The parlor creates an intimate, fluid boundary between the entry porch and the rear veranda. An elegant yet comfortable theme prevails throughout the home, with immediate transitions to outside living areas from the public rooms. A gallery connecting the stair hall with the great room and kitchen sports a niche with a built-in glass cabinet for mementos.

rear pool view |

An enchanting blend of seaside finesse and colonial charm, the waterfront home extends toward Gordon's Pass—an inland waterway a mere stone's throw from the Gulf of Mexico—in graduating levels from the rear veranda. The pool and spa area lead up to an alfresco dining space as well as down to the dock and harbor. A lanai accessed from the upstairs guest suites follows the extended perimeter of the home and offers wide-open views to visitors.

study | Exposed trusses iterate the symmetry and informality of the plan in the study. Tall windows and transoms frame a set of French doors that lead to a balcony and upper lanai facing the water. Paneled doors flanking the entertainment center lead to hall storage and to a bonus guest suite.

great room | Comfortable and elegant, the great room opens on both sides to the veranda and solana via sets of retractable French doors, providing a free flow of traffic to the sitting area, fireplace, and outdoor kitchen.

rear view | Fully engaged with the landscape, the rear perimeter borders an informal sitting area and grants panoramic vistas of Gordon's Pass. Grillwork lining the balcony above the leisure room expresses a regional influence, adapted from early revival styles of the late 19th Century. A walkway circumnavigates the pool and leads to the harbor and pier. Beyond the colonnade that lines the leisure room, a bay window provides captivating views for the master suite.

kitchen | Uniquely situated at the foot of the main stairwell at the front of the home, the gallery-style kitchen overlooks the leisure room and enjoys wide vistas of the rear property and harbor. A transitional space between the parlor and casual living area, the culinary kitchen features open counters intersected by passageways that increase circulation to the adjoining wings. Light ceilings and dark-wood cabinetry create an eclectic palette that is unified by marble counter-tops and a stone floor.

Sanabria | SATER TODAY

rear view | Embraced by views of the water, the veranda creates an idyllic setting for outdoor occasions—including family meals and gatherings—and connects the leisure room with the poolside areas. Stone pavers unify the outside spaces with the casual yet elegant theme of the home.

site plan | Within the limits of a narrow lot, this Floridian villa satisfies the owners' desire for a sense of the wide-open spaces and panoramic vistas of the sea. The rear perimeter opens to an expansive outdoor living area that straddles an infinity-edge pool and leads to the pier on the inland waterway. Retractable French doors create seamless boundaries between the casual living zone and the outside retreats, including a sitting area with a fireplace, and an alfresco kitchen. The entry parlor serves as an easy connection to the veranda, which permits access from virtually every room on the main level. The upper level includes a study and bonus room and two guest suites that share the lanai.

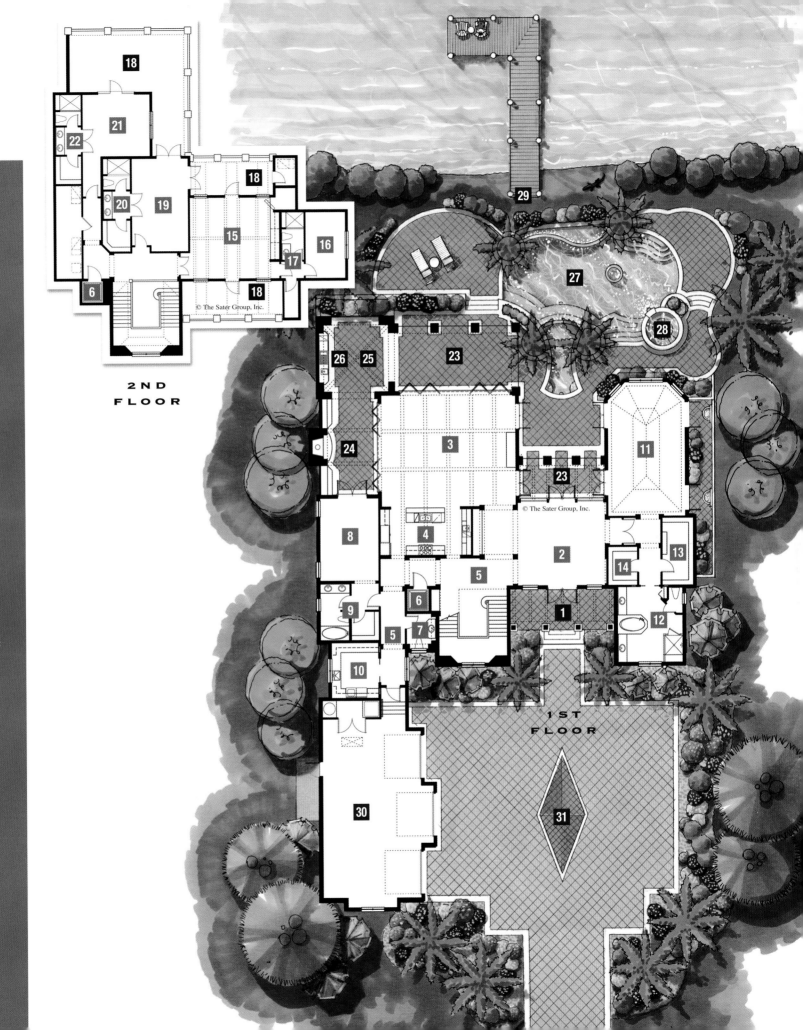

2ND FLOOR

1ST FLOOR

© The Sater Group, Inc.

© The Sater Group, Inc.

SATER CONCEPT

WHAT LIES AHEAD

Great houses of tomorrow

The grand experiment in residential architecture has not ended for The Sater Group—it has only begun. New, more adventurous works extend beyond planning interior space and developing fresh exterior styles to achieving a deeper understanding of the lifestyles of those who reside in the finished home. In Sater homes of the future, context is vital. Plans that focus on informal living, for example, include transitions to outdoor zones that are architecturally seamless, and engage strategies that ease the change of function from room to room.

To The Sater Group, good design means integrating traditional concepts with the smart amenities of a flexible floor plan. Advanced materials and capabilities play a more vital role in the house of tomorrow, and it is hard to imagine a household—even today—that does not rely heavily on technology for even the most basic tasks. How a house functions, how rooms flow into one another—even in complex arrangements—are not elements that are left to chance.

© THE SATER GROUP, INC.

new concepts | Time-honored compositions of scale and proportion provide a familiar, even historic, context for the unprecedented comforts that make our lives easier. For Dan Sater, the 21st-century home is classic in form and expresses simplicity in satisfying ways, with toned-down formal spaces, free-flowing interiors and open views that bring in swaths of scenery and a sense of nature.

The Sater Group's legacy continues with published works in countless books and magazines, thousands of plan sales nationally and internationally, and a rich and varied portfolio of designs. At last counting, the firm has garnered more than 350 prestigious design awards. However, the greatest testament to Dan's design influence is the large list of clients and customers worldwide who are pleased to reside in and enjoy a Sater home.

221

Multi-level Mediterranean homes create a superb waterfront community.

dan's notes | *With several designs working together in a collective project, the appeal of the streetscape is affected by the degree to which the individual houses relate to one another. In creating this palette of architectural styles, I found a common aesthetic in the Mediterranean vocabularies—with stone surrounds, vaulted entries and layered façades—that also works well in a waterfront locale. More importantly, I wanted to create a configuration of plans that would share common space and come together effectively as a neighborhood. Each design takes in views and offers an array of modern amenities, yet I feel that the true value of the project lies in its capacity to function as a community.*

beach project | Clustered around a splendid common area on narrow lots oriented toward the Gulf of Mexico, these beach-property houses take on the informality of their locale, yet are designed with grand floor plans and intricate exteriors that create a sense of elegance by the sea. Each unique architectural style complements the community motif as well as the attributes of the existing neighborhood, and is designed to harmonize with the detailed aesthetics of the surrounding plans. With ground-level entries that link to decks, bonus rooms and parking, the homes are designed to take full advantage of the property, with vertical arrangements of living levels that improve function and maximize views. Dual mezzanine levels accommodate traditional living spaces—such as the great room, dining area and kitchen on the lower story, and guest quarters and recreation rooms above—while the top levels are dedicated to luxe private retreats.

LOCATION:
BAREFOOT BEACH, FLORIDA

LANDSCAPE ARCHITECT:
OUTSIDE PRODUCTIONS, INC.

front and rear views | The ground-level entry exhibits the character and beauty of Italian Renaissance villas, with such features as rusticated surrounds, metallic sconces and vaulted arches. Varied window treatments indicate a 19th-century influence, and an upper-level arcaded porch complements the theme. Layered massing subdues the vertical dimensions of the elevation, with hosts of windows and sculpted niches lending a sense of texture and depth to the façade. At the rear of the plan, a veranda defined by a massive colonnade anchors three levels of outdoor areas, including a double portico and an observation deck accessed from the top-level master suite.

Veronica | SATER CONCEPT

4 BEDROOM
4-1/2 BATH
7,483 SQ. FT.
LIVING AREA

© THE SATER GROUP, INC.

Esplanade | SATER CONCEPT

4 BEDROOM
4 FULL BATHS
2 HALF BATHS
7,518 SQ. FT.
LIVING AREA

front view | A pedestrian-friendly approach enhances the streetscape and leads to the grand, vaulted entry of this Mediterranean-style design. Decorative brackets highlight an impressive glass turret and a center gable set off by a quatrefoil transom, which brings natural light to the second mezzanine level.

© THE SATER GROUP, INC.

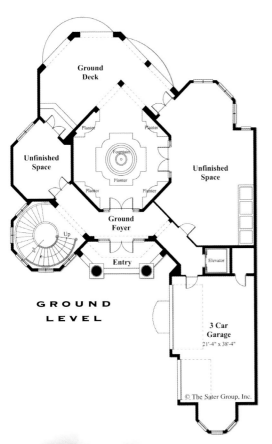

GROUND LEVEL

Ground Deck

Unfinished Space

Fountain

Planter

Ground Foyer

Planter

Unfinished Space

Up

Entry

Elevator

3 Car Garage
21'-4" x 38'-4"

© The Sater Group, Inc.

1ST FLOOR

© The Sater Group, Inc.

Veranda 1
22'-0" x 26'-0"

Fireplace

Built-In

Study
16'-0" x 13'-8"
14'-2" Clg.

Two-Sided Fireplace

Grand Room
22'-0" x 22'-0"
12'-0"-14'-2" Clg.

Dining Room
15'-4" x 17'-0"
14'-2" Clg.

Wet Bar

Wine Cellar

Arch

Kitchen
20'-3" x 16'-0"
14'-2" Clg.

Fr. Ref.

Ovens

Mezzanine 1
14'-2" Clg.

Down

Up

Mezzanine Balcony

Arch

Elevator

Butler's Pantry

Arch

Powder Bath 1

Gallery

Linen

Seat

Walk-In Shower

Bath 1

W.I.C.

Guest Suite 1
13'-2" x 14'-10"
12'-8" Clg.

Sitting
11'-2" x 9'-8"
12'-8" Clg.

© The Sater Group, Inc.

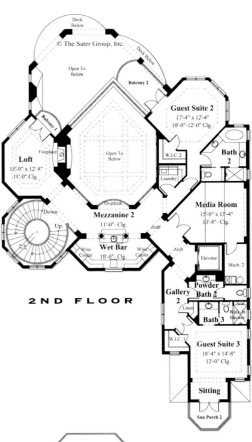

2ND FLOOR

© The Sater Group, Inc.

Deck Below

Open To Below

Balcony 2

Guest Suite 2
17'-4" x 12'-4"
10'-0"-12'-0" Clg.

Balcony 1

Loft
15'-0" x 12'-8"
11'-0" Clg.

Fireplace

W.I.C. 2

Bath 2

Open To Below

Laundry

Media Room
15'-0" x 15'-4"
13'-8" Clg.

Overlook

Down

Up

Mezzanine 2
11'-0" Clg.

Arch

Wine Cooler

Wet Bar
10'-0" Clg.

Wine Cooler

Arch

Elevator

Mech. 2

Gallery 2

Powder Bath 2

Linen

Seat

Walk-In Shower

Bath 3

W.I.C.

Guest Suite 3
18'-4" x 14'-8"
12'-0" Clg.

Sitting

Sun Porch 2

spaces

Living Ground	535
Living One	2,839
Living Two	2,372
Living Three	1,772
Total Living	**7,518**
Veranda One	633
Balc./Porch One	87
Balc./Porch Two	196
Deck Three	575
Garage	838
Entry	153
TOTAL	**10,000**

3RD FLOOR

Master Sundeck

Master Loggia
12'-0" Clg.

Dressing

Tub

Her Bath

Built-In

Vestibule

Linen

Fireplace

Master Suite
23'-4" x 20'-4"
12'-0"-13'-0" Clg.

Built-In

Juice Bar

Walk-In Shower

Seat

W.I.C.

His Bath

Down

Mech. Room

Master Foyer

Utility

Elevator

Mech. Chase

© The Sater Group, Inc.

rear view | Designed as a getaway retreat, the plan boasts four levels of outdoor living areas at the rear perimeter, with a wide veranda, loggia and deck oriented toward the Gulf of Mexico. Large, informal living spaces create a flexible arrangement for owners who entertain guests and family, and complement private retreats on all three levels.

Marcellina | SATER CONCEPT

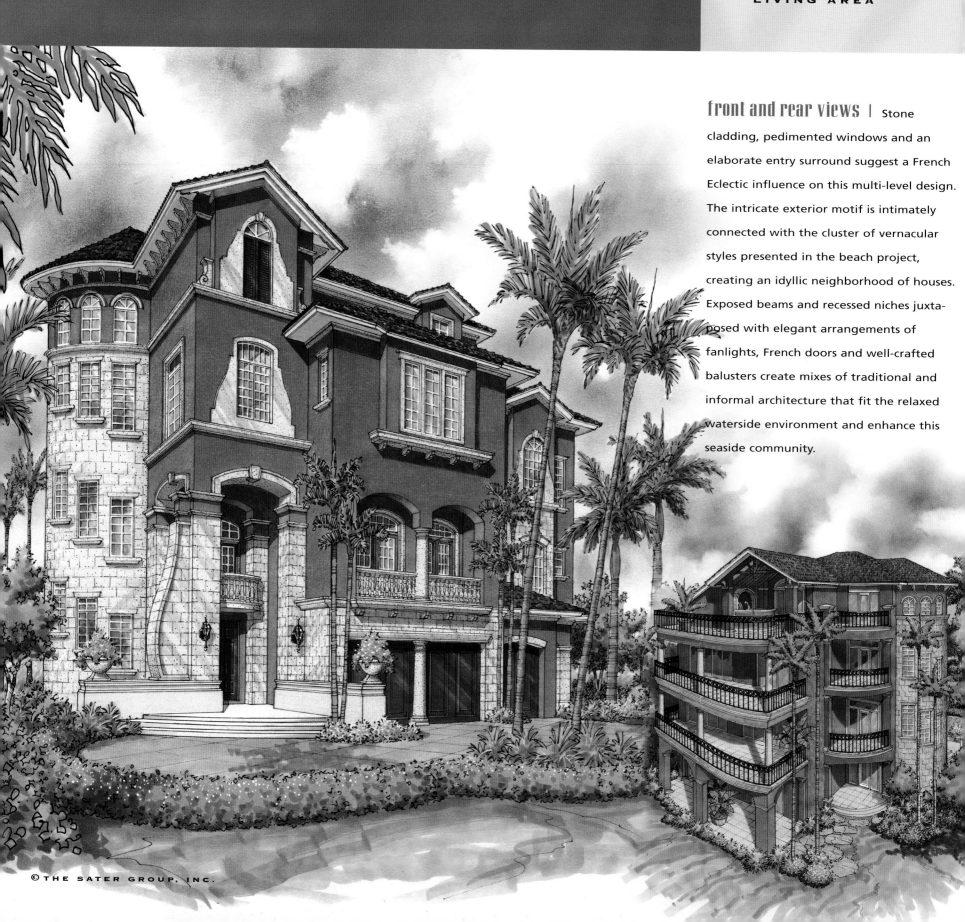

front and rear views | Stone cladding, pedimented windows and an elaborate entry surround suggest a French Eclectic influence on this multi-level design. The intricate exterior motif is intimately connected with the cluster of vernacular styles presented in the beach project, creating an idyllic neighborhood of houses. Exposed beams and recessed niches juxtaposed with elegant arrangements of fanlights, French doors and well-crafted balusters create mixes of traditional and informal architecture that fit the relaxed waterside environment and enhance this seaside community.

© THE SATER GROUP, INC.

site plan legend

1 ESPLANADE

2 MARCELLINA

3 VERONICA

4 PUTTING GREEN

5 COMMON POOL
  & AMENITIES

6 EXISTING HOMES

7 BOARDWALK

8 COMMON AREA

site plan | Three distinct exterior styles—neo-Mediterranean, Italian Renaissance and French Eclectic—create a harmonious streetscape within this beachfront development. With multi-level living areas oriented to the rear perimeters, the cluster houses achieve panoramic views that extend beyond the common areas to the Gulf of Mexico. At the center of the site, the putting green, pool and boardwalk connect the individual residences with a sense of community and enhance the quality of everyday life by the sea.

© The Sater Group, Inc.

227

Rutledge | SATER CONCEPT

3 BEDROOM
3 FULL BATHS
3 HALF BATHS
7,472 SQ. FT.
LIVING AREA

© THE SATER GROUP, INC.

FRONT ELEVATION

front elevation |

Stone and wood shingles merge beautifully with contemporary elements on this Neo-Shingle lakeside villa, with classic columns and clapboard siding evoking the past. A uniquely contemporary adaptation of the traditional Shingle cottage borrows sculpted shapes and curved towers from its traditional precedents. Here, the free-form cottage look is transformed into an organic style, with a grandeur and freshness that suits the splendid waterfront site. Rows of windows and transoms admit ample natural light to the interior and, throughout the home, bring in panoramas of scenery. The standing-seam roof on the central turret is strikingly combined with hipped rooflines and time-honored mixes of gables and dormers on this 21st-century home.

228

ENTRY RENDERING

© THE SATER GROUP, INC.

REAR RENDERING

rear and front views | Framed by bayed turrets, the formal entry overlooks the terraced garden at the front of the home, with rows of muntin windows lining the façade. A cupola caps a rotunda encircled by a row of clerestory windows, which bring daylight into a study with views of the river. At the rear perimeter, the central tower features floor-to-ceiling windows that permit wide vistas of the waterfront property, and access to a private balcony. To the right, a Florida room features an outdoor fireplace and conversation seating sheltered by a classic arcade.

229

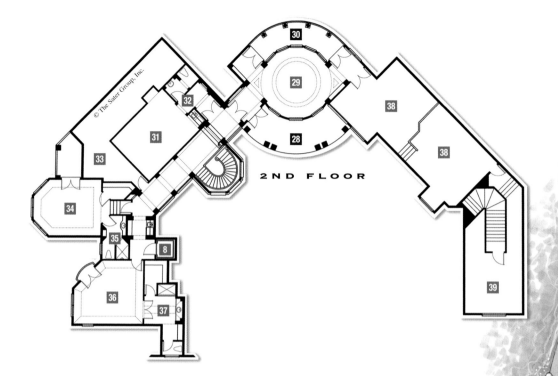

2ND FLOOR

© The Sater Group, Inc.

site plan | A progressive approach from the motor court to the main entry leads through a lush terraced garden framed by bay turrets. The grand foyer presents an interior vista of the splendid rear property—a wide girth of land jutting into the river—marked only with walkways leading down to the water. To the left of the plan, a capacious great room links to the aptly named "Florida Room" via French doors, and features a sitting nook, corner fireplace and wet bar. A formal dining bay is open to the kitchen, which provides access to the library and solarium. The central stairs lead to an upper-level gallery, media room, study and guest quarters. On the main floor, a vestibule sentinels the entrance to a secluded master suite, which includes separate wardrobes, a bumped-out whirlpool tub surrounded by a garden and fountain, and private access to the rear deck and pool.

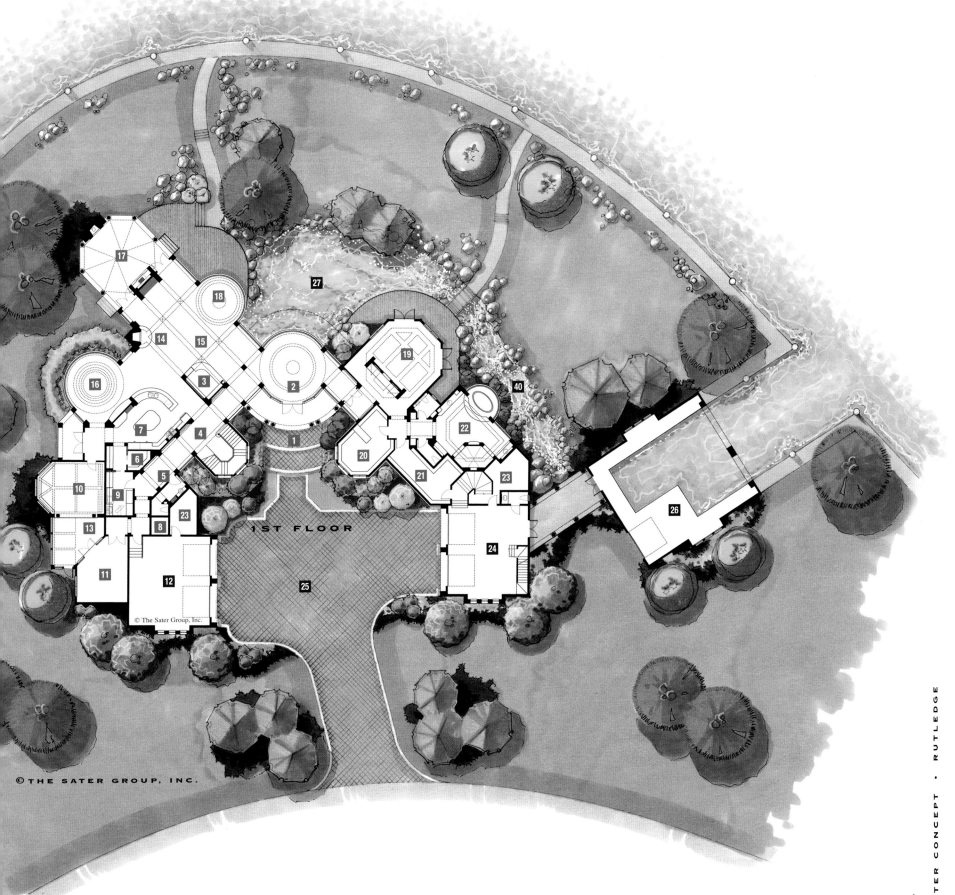

1ST FLOOR

© The Sater Group, Inc.

©THE SATER GROUP, INC.

© THE SATER GROUP, INC.

FRONT PERSPECTIVE

front entry view | A propylaeum-style gateway marks the entrance to the splendid forecourt of this grand Mediterranean villa, sited on the banks of the Caloosahatchee River. Massive stone piers announce a deeply recessed entry, framed by two guest casitas, which provide individual entries just inside the gate. Situated on a wide lot, the footprint of the home expands well beyond the perimeter of the forward structures, with a wide exposure to waterfront views at the rear elevation.

Authentic details such as the rusticated surround of the entry gate, decorative overhanging eaves, and cross-beamed shutters articulate the period theme of the home, and complement the interior's elegant design. Spacious rooms, made glorious by stunning riverfront views and intimate links to the outdoors, establish a refined character for the plan and set off a series of lanais and verandas defining the property.

front elevation | Characterized by evocative elements of Venetian architecture, the streetscape presents a highly ornate Italian Renaissance vocabulary. Rich with picturesque combinations of arches, balusters and ornamented windows, the layered elevation integrates historic components with a subtropical environment—creating an exotic retreat well suited to its locale. The tallest of the central towers harbors an observatory with a wrapping deck, an outdoor sanctuary which offers scenic panoramas of the riverfront. To the right of the plan, upper and lower guest suites above the garage offer privacy for the owners' friends and family.

courtyard view | Within the entry gates, a processional approach to the formal entry encompasses a koi pond and main pool—which wraps the cantilevered bay harboring the exercise room. Double doors lead to a magnificent rotunda inside the central tower.

COURTYARD VIEW

Matteucci | SATER CONCEPT

7 BEDROOM
7 FULL BATHS
3 HALF BATHS
12,277 SQ. FT.
LIVING AREA

© THE SATER GROUP, INC.

COURTYARD VIEW

courtyard view | Vistas extend from the grotto and front veranda the length of the pool to the spa and fountain. An exquisite exercise bay cantilevers over the water, with floor-to-ceiling windows that offer a vast panorama of the courtyard. A gazebo near the spa serves as a terminus to a walkway that leads from the master wing, which features a rambling bath with room-sized closets and a whirlpool tub enclosed in a space that opens to a private garden. Above the grotto, the upper-level bay harbors the wife's secluded study and a chapel for prayer. On the opposite side of the courtyard, a spacious outdoor kitchen and dining area offers views of the pool.

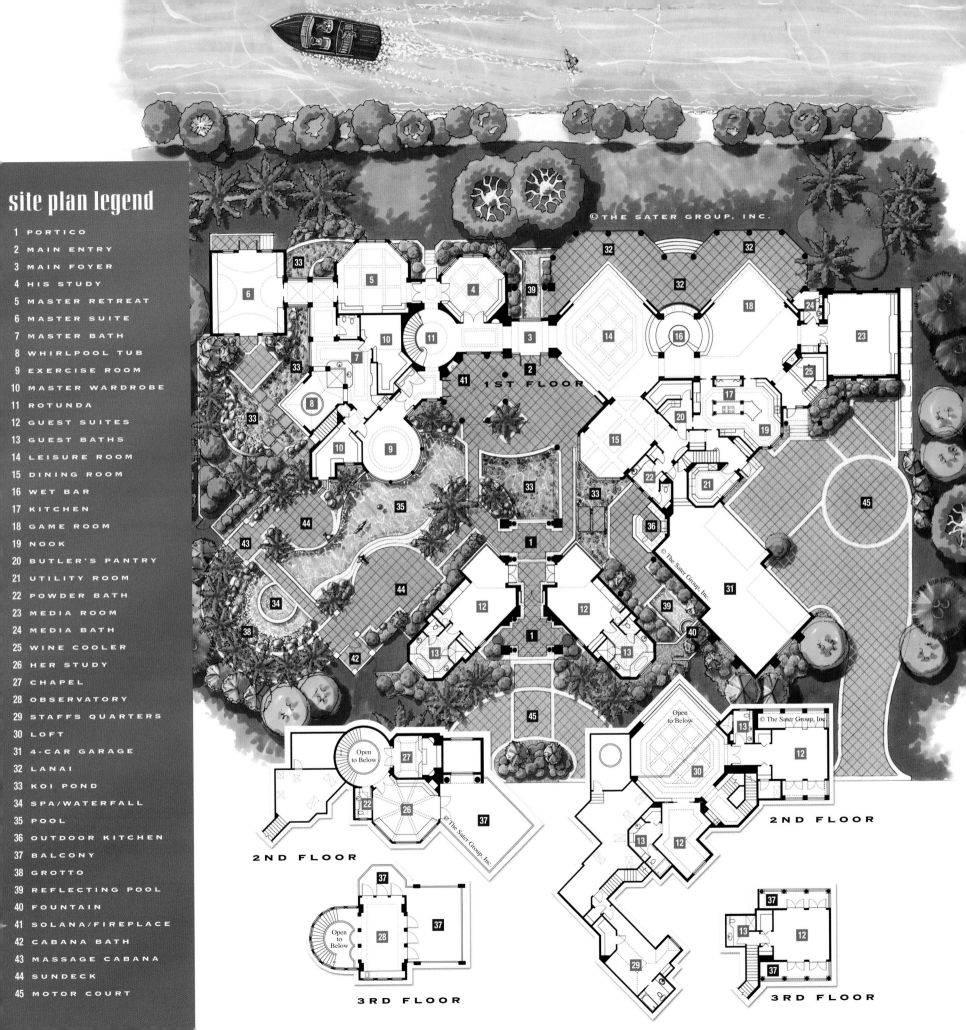

site plan legend

1 PORTICO
2 MAIN ENTRY
3 MAIN FOYER
4 HIS STUDY
5 MASTER RETREAT
6 MASTER SUITE
7 MASTER BATH
8 WHIRLPOOL TUB
9 EXERCISE ROOM
10 MASTER WARDROBE
11 ROTUNDA
12 GUEST SUITES
13 GUEST BATHS
14 LEISURE ROOM
15 DINING ROOM
16 WET BAR
17 KITCHEN
18 GAME ROOM
19 NOOK
20 BUTLER'S PANTRY
21 UTILITY ROOM
22 POWDER BATH
23 MEDIA ROOM
24 MEDIA BATH
25 WINE COOLER
26 HER STUDY
27 CHAPEL
28 OBSERVATORY
29 STAFFS QUARTERS
30 LOFT
31 4-CAR GARAGE
32 LANAI
33 KOI POND
34 SPA/WATERFALL
35 POOL
36 OUTDOOR KITCHEN
37 BALCONY
38 GROTTO
39 REFLECTING POOL
40 FOUNTAIN
41 SOLANA/FIREPLACE
42 CABANA BATH
43 MASSAGE CABANA
44 SUNDECK
45 MOTOR COURT

© THE SATER GROUP, INC.

1ST FLOOR

© The Sater Group, Inc.

2ND FLOOR

© The Sater Group, Inc.

2ND FLOOR

3RD FLOOR

3RD FLOOR

Monterra | SATER CONCEPT

© THE SATER GROUP, INC.

FRONT PERSEPECTIVE

front view | Encircled by a motor court, a central fountain welcomes visitors to this Italian-style villa. A strong sense of detail evocative of 16th-century Venetian architecture defines the streetscape, with a generous display of windows and outside spaces lining the façade. A cupola rises above the roofline, capping a dome ceiling that enhances the ornate master bath. Carved-stone balustrades, arched colonnades and a bold central entry with a rusticated surround articulate the historic Mediterranean theme, and create an inviting approach to the home.

site plan | A stunning porte-cochere links the motor court to the secondary garage, which offers access to the home via a service entrance that connects a cluster of informal rooms surrounding the kitchen. A sizeable pantry area, gallery and nook facilitate planned events, while the formal dining room features a splendid bay window. Beyond the entry, the foyer offers a spectacular rotunda ceiling and leads to an impressive gallery and circular stairwell that connects to a balcony bridge. An informal wing includes a media room and access to the courtyard through the casual living area.

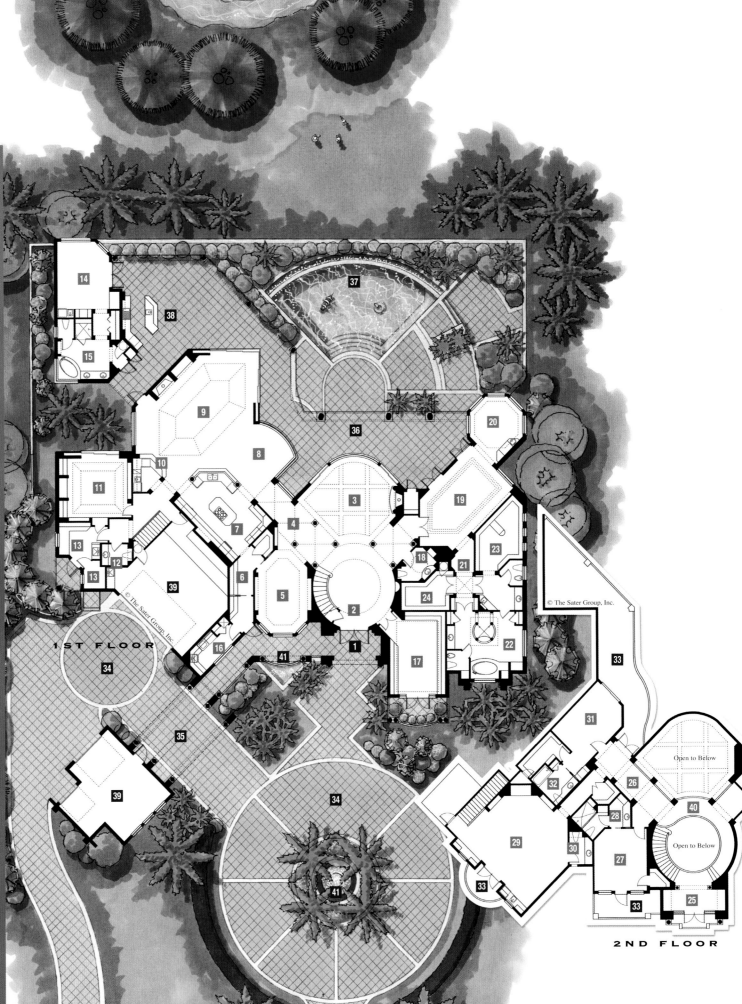

1ST FLOOR

© The Sater Group, Inc.

2ND FLOOR

Open to Below

Open to Below

Bradbury | SATER CONCEPT

© THE SATER GROUP, INC.

FRONT VIEW

front view | Strong traditional lines define the streetscape of this Mediterranean-style manor. Carved brackets line deeply overhanging eaves and a classic arcade surrounds the recessed entry. Fanlights and hipped rooflines distinguish the historic elements of the façade, with a pronounced referenced to the architectural forms of the Italian Renaissance.

rear view | Sited on a steeply sloped lot, the plan visually integrates a cascading water element into the natural rock formations of the cliffs leading down to the lake.

REAR VIEW

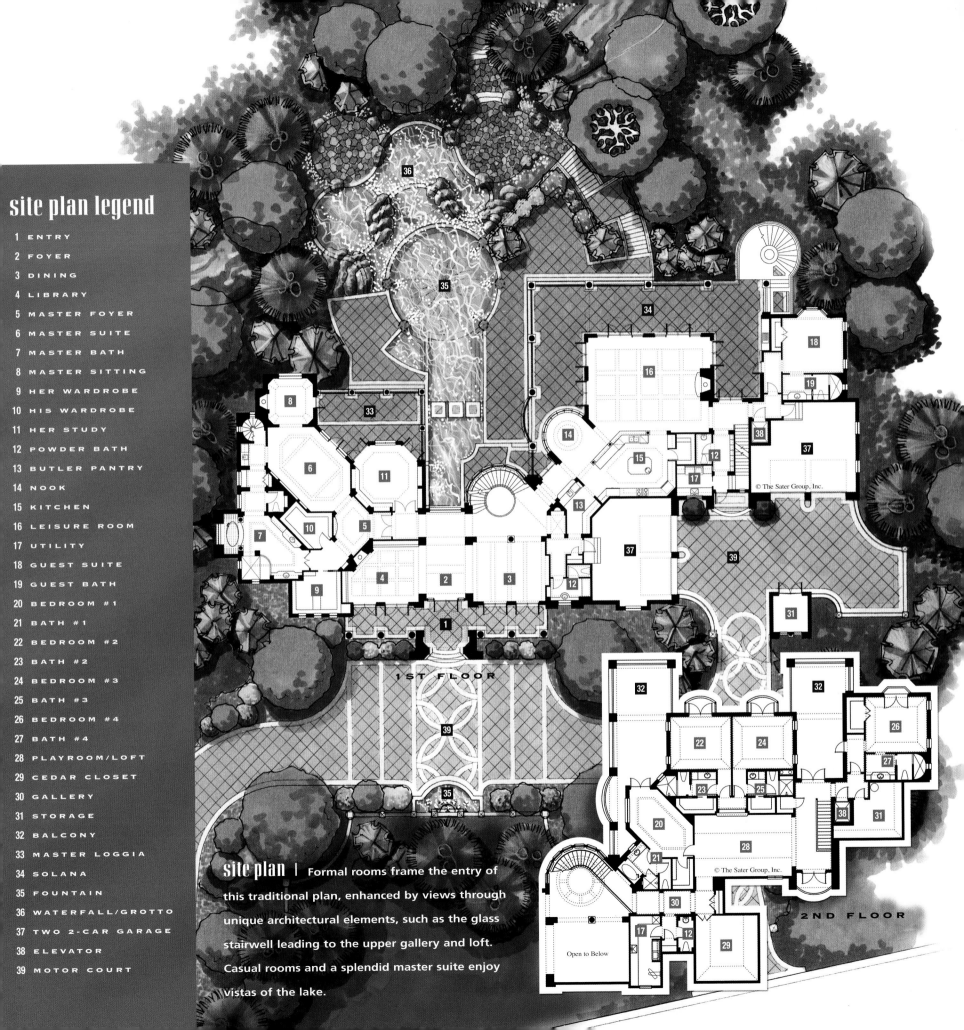

site plan legend

1 ENTRY
2 FOYER
3 DINING
4 LIBRARY
5 MASTER FOYER
6 MASTER SUITE
7 MASTER BATH
8 MASTER SITTING
9 HER WARDROBE
10 HIS WARDROBE
11 HER STUDY
12 POWDER BATH
13 BUTLER PANTRY
14 NOOK
15 KITCHEN
16 LEISURE ROOM
17 UTILITY
18 GUEST SUITE
19 GUEST BATH
20 BEDROOM #1
21 BATH #1
22 BEDROOM #2
23 BATH #2
24 BEDROOM #3
25 BATH #3
26 BEDROOM #4
27 BATH #4
28 PLAYROOM/LOFT
29 CEDAR CLOSET
30 GALLERY
31 STORAGE
32 BALCONY
33 MASTER LOGGIA
34 SOLANA
35 FOUNTAIN
36 WATERFALL/GROTTO
37 TWO 2-CAR GARAGE
38 ELEVATOR
39 MOTOR COURT

1ST FLOOR

© The Sater Group, Inc.

2ND FLOOR

Open to Below

© The Sater Group, Inc.

site plan | Formal rooms frame the entry of this traditional plan, enhanced by views through unique architectural elements, such as the glass stairwell leading to the upper gallery and loft. Casual rooms and a splendid master suite enjoy vistas of the lake.

© THE SATER GROUP, INC.

FRONT ELEVATION

front elevation |

Slated for a deep lot with a narrow waterfront exposure, this contemporary design merges experimental elements with a tranquil seaside character. Conceived as a showcase home for Microsun corporate staff and clients, the inventive plan offers a streetscape that is both coolly modern and engagingly familiar. Strong, sweeping lines define the perimeter, which hugs the bay shore and integrates distinctive water features throughout the property. Inside, the design celebrates the notion of home with traditional features that promote function, and innovative traits—such as a series of halide lamps and canlights that enliven the classical context of the architecture. Historic influences, such as the entry turret, keystone arches and robust piers of the façade, complement the fresh lines and stunning curves of the outer plan.

water features | A koi pond wraps the core of the perimeter, in varied forms that enhance the exterior and even the interior structure of the plan. At the central gallery, a vestibule with a groin-vaulted ceiling features a glass floor with views of the koi pond running underneath the home. Mounted on the exterior wall outside of the kitchen, dual fountains feed the stream and water-fall formed by the steady surge of water that leads from the bayside elevation.

rear elevation | Facing the bay, the rear perimeter is designed to take in views of the water and relate to the landscape in ways that subdue the edgier, new-century aspects of the home. A linear approach to the curved footprint offers satisfying transitions from the formal and casual spaces to the outdoor zones.

FRONT POND VIEW

REAR ELEVATION

Rockwell | SATER CONCEPT

4 BEDROOM
4 FULL BATHS
2 HALF BATHS
7,495 SQ. FT.
LIVING AREA

© THE SATER GROUP, INC.

GREAT ROOM VIEW

site plan legend

1 ENTRY
2 FOYER
3 GREAT ROOM
4 FIREPLACE
5 DINING
6 KITCHEN
7 BUTLER'S PANTRY
8 BREAKFAST NOOK
9 LEISURE ROOM
10 POWDER BATH
11 UTILITY
12 MASTER SUITE
13 MASTER BATH
14 MASTER CLOSET
15 LIBRARY
16 POOL BATH
17 GUEST SUITE #1
18 GUEST BATH #1
19 GUEST SUITE #2
20 GUEST BATH #2
21 GUEST SUITE #3
22 GUEST BATH #3
23 OUTDOOR KITCHEN
24 OUTDOOR FIREPLACE
25 LANAI
26 POOL
27 SPA
28 2-CAR GARAGE
29 PORTE-COCHERE
30 GUEST LANAI
31 KOI POND
32 FOUNTAINS
33 PUTTING GREEN
34 PERGOLA
35 SUN DECK
36 GUEST MOTOR COURT
37 MOTOR COURT

great room | A cross-beam ceiling and rusticated chimney offer a sense of intimacy to a living space designed with wall-mounted 21st-century lights fed by fiber optics. French doors open the space to the pool and spa area.

site plan | Thoroughly engaged with the landscape, the design incorporates a stream linking two koi ponds into the interior plan. At the vestibule that defines the public and private areas, a glass floor permits views of the water running under the property. The plan allows a highly functional interior to flow seamlessly between informal spaces and rooms designated for business-related occasions. Clustered guest suites and a rambling master suite frame the lanai and pool, and offer private patios.

34

33

35

19

20

36

27

18

30

26

17

32

16

15

13

24

14

4

23

25

25

3

32

12

9

8

29

Glass Floor

Curved Cupola Above

2

© The Sater Group, Inc.

10

6

31

5

1

11

1ST
FLOOR

7

© The Sater Group, Inc.

21

22

31

2ND
FLOOR

37

28

29

32

sater early years

WATERFORD
Bonita Springs, FL
1993
Pages 16-23

Builder:
Lifestyle Concepts
Landscape Architect:
Smallwood Design Group
Interior Designer: Richard Geary Interiors
Photographer: Oscar Thompson

Awards: 1993 Sand Dollar Awards: Best Super
Luxury Home, Best Sitescaping, Best Curb Appeal;
1993 Lee Building Industry — Product Design of
the Year for a Home over $700,000

MARISKA
Naples, FL
1992
Pages 24-29

Builder:
London Bay Homes
Landscape Architect:
Smallwood Design Group,
Scott Windham, ASLA
Interior Designer: Jan Wallace, Robb & Stucky
Photographer: Oscar Thompson

Awards: 1992 AIBD Designers' Choice Award and
Best of Show; 1992 Pinnacle Awards —
Best Custom Design over $700,000;
1993 AIBD Design Awards: First Place —
Custom Luxury Homes and Best Custom Home
over $700,000

ALCHEMIE
Greenville, OH
1993
Pages 30-35

Builder:
Dale Rismiller
Landscape Architect:
Smallwood Design Group, Scott Windham, ASLA
Interior Designer: Robb & Stucky
Photographer: Bill Swartz

Awards: 1993 AIBD 2nd Place: Custom Luxury Home
1993 Aurora Awards Best Custom Home;
1993 Florida Residential Design Association —
1st Place: Custom Luxury;
1995 AIBD Designer's Choice Award

sater 90's

WINDSOR
Naples, FL
1995
Pages 38-45

Builder:
Lifestyle Concepts, Inc.
Landscape Architect:
Smallwood Design Group
Interior Designer: Naples Design Collection
Photographer: Laurence Taylor & Oscar Thompson

Awards: 1996 Aurora Awards — Best Single Family
Home $2 million and over, and Best Bath in a
Single Family Home over $1 million.

MILANO
Marco Island, FL
1997
Pages 46-53

Builder:
Slocum Christian
Landscape Architect:
Smallwood Design Group,
Scott Windham, ASLA
Interior Designer: Marc Michaels Interiors
Photographer: Laurence Taylor

Awards: 1997 Aurora Awards First Place: Custom
Luxury Home;
1997 Institute of Building Design
1st Place: Custom Luxury

McKENNA
Bonita Springs, FL
1998
Pages 54-59

Builder:
Lifestyle Concepts, Inc.
Landscape Architect:
W. Christian Busk
Interior Designer: Accessories Etc. Inc.,
Chrissie Forbs, ASID
Photographer: Laurence Taylor

Awards: 1999 AIBD Builder's Choice Award;
1999 AIBD 1st Place: Custom Luxury Home

SUMATRA
Bonita Springs, FL
1998
Pages 60-69

Builder:
Cronacher
Development Corp.
Landscape Architect:
W. Christian Busk
Interior Designer:
Accessories Etc., Inc., Chrissie Forbes, ASID
Photographer: Laurence Taylor

Awards: 1999 AIBD 2nd Place: Honor Award
of Excellence

VALLI
Bonita Springs, FL
1994
Pages 70-75

Builder:
Lifestyle Concepts, Inc.
Landscape Architect:
W. Christian Busk
Interior Designer: Lisa Lovetto
Photographer: Laurence Taylor

Awards: 1998 Aurora Awards First Place: Custom
Luxury Home;
1998 AIBD First Place: Custom Luxury Home

COACHELLA
Bonita Springs, FL
1996
Pages 76-85

Builder:
Portofino Homes
Landscape Architect:
Wilson Miller Associates,
Dennis Church, ASLA
Interior Designer:
Wanda Nelson, Decorating Preference
Photographer: CJ Walker

Not submitted for awards.

MIRADA
Naples, FL
1997
Pages 86-91

Builder:
Boran Craig Barber
Homes
Landscape Architect:
Smallwood Design Group
Interior Designer: Urban Studio Associates
Photographer: CJ Walker

Not submitted for awards.

sater today

CORDILLERA
Naples, FL
2005
Pages 94-109

Builder: Kurtz Homes
Landscape Architect:
Outside Productions, Inc.,
Scott Windham, ASLA
Interior Designer: Accessories Etc., Inc.
Photographer: CJ Walker

Not submitted for awards.

SEABROOK
Sanibel Island, FL
2004
Pages 110-121

Builder:
Benchmark Builders
Landscape:
R.S. Walsh Landscaping, Inc.
Interior Designer:
Robb & Stucky, Deborah Maurer, ASID
Photographer: CJ Walker

Awards: 2004 Aurora Awards First Place;
2004 AIBD 1st Place: Custom Luxury Home

SALINA
Naples, FL
2003
Pages 122-131

Builder: Kurtz Homes
Landscape Architect:
Outside Productions, Inc.
Interior Designer:
Accessories Etc., Inc.
Photographer: CJ Walker

Awards: 2003 AIBD Designer's Choice;
Garlinghouse Designer's Choice

RAFINA
Naples, FL
2001
Pages 132-143

Builder: Kurtz Homes
Landscape Architect:
Outside Productions, Inc.,
Scott Windham, ASLA
Interior Designer: Accessories Etc., Inc.
Photographer: CJ Walker

Not submitted for awards.

HARMON
Boca Grande, FL
2003
Pages 144-153

Builder: Safety Harbor
Homes, Inc.
Landscape Architect:
Outside Productions, Inc.
Scott Windham, ASLA
Interior Designer: Myrna Garbins Designs
Photographer: CJ Walker

Awards: 2004 AIBD Honor Award of Excellence:
Custom Luxury Home

BELISIMA
Naples, FL
2002
Pages 154-165

Builder:
Hunt Construction
Landscape Architect:
Fairview Landscape
Interior Designer: Vince Muller & Associates
Photographer: Joseph Lapeyra

Awards: 2003 AIBD & Garlinghouse 2nd Place:
Honor Award of Excellence

PIETRA MAR
Sanibel Island, FL
1997
Pages 166-177

Builder:
The Wolter Group
Landscape Architect:
Smallwood Design
Group, Scott Windham, ASLA
Interior Designer: Marc Michaels Interiors
Photographer: Laurence Taylor

Awards: 1999 AIBD 2nd Place: Award of Excellence

MALYA
Marco Island, FL
2004
Pages 178-183

Builder:
Snell Construction
Landscape Architect:
Outside Productions, Inc.
Interior Designer:
David L. Smith Interiors, Gary Clark
Photographer: CJ Walker

Not submitted for awards.

VILLORESI
Marco Island, Florida
2004
Pages 184-195

Builder:
Snell Construction
Landscape Architect:
Outside Productions, Inc.,
Scott Windham, ASLA
Interior Designer: David L. Smith
Photographer: CJ Walker

Not submitted for awards.

FIORENTINO
Naples, FL
2000
Pages 196-201

Builder: Harbourside
Custom Homes
Landscape Architect:
Outside Productions, Inc.
Interior Designer: Freestyle Interiors
Photographer: Dan Forer

Awards: 2001 Aurora Awards Best in State for
Single-Family Detached Home over $3 million;
2001 AIBD Designer's Choice Award and Honor
Award of Excellence: Custom Luxury Design

ALAMOSA
Naples, FL
2003
Pages 202-211

Builder:
Hourborside Custom
Homes
Landscape Architect:
Outside Productions, Inc., Pat Trefz, ASLA
Interior Designer: Vogue Interiors,
Debbie DiMaria
Photographer: Michael Lowry

Awards: 2003 LBIA Parade of Homes Merit
Award: Best Architectural Design

SANABRIA
Naples, FL
2005
Pages 212-219

Builder: Kurtz Homes
Landscape Architect:
Russell P. Bencaz &
Associates, Inc.
Interior Designer: Nancy Ruzicka
Photographer: CJ Walker

Not submitted for awards.

sater concept — beach project

sater concept

VERONICA
BAREFOOT BEACH
PROJECT
Bonita Beach, FL
2005
Pages 222-223

Landscape Architect:
Outside Productions, Inc.
Renderer: Dave Jenkins

ESPLANADE
BAREFOOT BEACH
PROJECT
Bonita Beach, FL
2005
Pages 224-225

Landscape Architect:
Outside Productions, Inc.
Renderer: Dave Jenkins

MARCELLINA
BAREFOOT BEACH
PROJECT
Bonita Beach, FL
2005
Pages 226-227

Landscape Architect:
Outside Productions, Inc.
Renderer: Dave Jenkins

RUTLEDGE
St. Joseph, MI
2001
Pages 228-231

Landscape Architect:
Christian Andrea
Renderer: Dave Jenkins

MATTEUCCI
Ft. Myers, FL
2000
Pages 232-235

Builder: Lifestyle Concepts, Inc.
Interior Design: William E. Clements, ASID
Renderer: Dave Jenkins

MONTERRA
Naples, FL
1998
Pages 236-237

Builder:
Boran Craig Barber and Engel Construction, Inc.
Landscape Architect: Smallwood Design Group
Renderer: Dave Jenkins

BRADBURY
Raleigh, NC
2005
Pages 238-239

Builder: Mike Young
Landscape Architect:
Windham Studios, Scott Windham, ASLA
Renderer: Dave Jenkins

ROCKWELL
Bonita Springs, FL
1997
Pages 240-243

Builder: Hunt Construction
Landscape Architect:
Smallwood Design Group
Interior Design: Marc Michaels Interiors
Renderer: Dave Jenkins

Index

The satisfaction of creating beautiful homes

for my clients has been an essential part of my life and career.

As I reflect on my professional journey, I acknowledge being blessed with clients

eager to be a part of my concept and philosophy of reinventing the home.

After all, designing the perfect home is like a marriage:

the arrangement must compliment each partner and offer an appreciation

of the function of everyday life in order to make it all work.

Many may respond differently to my designs.

In the end, though, a home's merit is determined by how well it serves

its owners and its site—that is what matters most to me.

— Dan F. Sater II, AIBD